Cambridge Elements ☰

Elements in Beckett Studies
edited by
Dirk Van Hulle
University of Oxford
Mark Nixon
University of Reading

SAMUEL BECKETT AND CULTURAL NATIONALISM

Shane Weller

University of Kent

CAMBRIDGE
UNIVERSITY PRESS

CAMBRIDGE
UNIVERSITY PRESS

University Printing House, Cambridge CB2 8BS, United Kingdom

One Liberty Plaza, 20th Floor, New York, NY 10006, USA

477 Williamstown Road, Port Melbourne, VIC 3207, Australia

314–321, 3rd Floor, Plot 3, Splendor Forum, Jasola District Centre,
New Delhi – 110025, India

79 Anson Road, #06–04/06, Singapore 079906

Cambridge University Press is part of the University of Cambridge.

It furthers the University's mission by disseminating knowledge in the pursuit of
education, learning, and research at the highest international levels of excellence.

www.cambridge.org
Information on this title: www.cambridge.org/9781009045483
DOI: 10.1017/9781009042277

First published 2021

A catalogue record for this publication is available from the British Library.

ISBN 978-1-009-04548-3 Paperback
ISSN 2632-0746 (online)
ISSN 2632-0738 (print)

Samuel Beckett and Cultural Nationalism

Elements in Beckett Studies

DOI: 10.1017/9781009042277
First published online: May 2021

Shane Weller
University of Kent

Author for correspondence: Shane Weller, S.J.Weller@kent.ac.uk

Abstract: Drawing on evidence from his published works, manuscripts, and correspondence, *Samuel Beckett and Cultural Nationalism* explores Beckett's engagement with the theme of cultural nationalism throughout his writing life, revealing the various ways in which he sought to challenge culturally nationalist conceptions of art and literature, while never embracing a cosmopolitan approach. The Element shows how, in his pre-Second World War writings, Beckett sought openly to mock Irish nationalist ideas of culture and language, but that, in so doing, he failed to avoid what he himself described as a 'clot of prejudices'. In his post-war works in French and English, however, following time spent in Nazi Germany in 1936–7 as well as in the French Resistance during the Second World War, Beckett began to take a new approach to ideas of national-cultural affiliation, at the heart of which was a conception of the human as a citizen of nowhere.

Keywords: nationalism, cosmopolitanism, Samuel Beckett, translation, violence

ISBNs: 9781009045483 (PB), 9781009042277 (OC)
ISSNs: 2632-0746 (online), 2632-0738 (print)

Contents

1 Introduction

When, after repeated frustrations and disappointments, Samuel Beckett's novel *Murphy* was finally published, on 7 March 1938, one might reasonably have anticipated that his reaction would have been a combination of pleasure and relief. After all, not only had this thirty-one-year-old writer's first completed novel, *Dream of Fair to Middling Women*, been roundly rejected by publishers six years earlier, but the number of publishing houses to have also turned down *Murphy* was considerable, as Beckett's own personal list of rejections testifies.[1] And yet, on receiving his author's copies of the book from George Routledge & Sons, Beckett immediately dispatched a letter to his close friend Thomas MacGreevy,[2] lamenting the colours chosen by the publisher for the book's dustjacket, which, he observed, was 'All green white & yellow'. These were, of course, the colours of the national flag of Ireland, which, following a referendum in July 1937, had in December of that year adopted a new constitution as Éire, replacing the former Saorstát Éireann (Irish Free State). Both the novel's title and the author's name were printed in green on the dustjacket, underlain by a large yellow 'R' for Routledge on a white base. Beckett's conclusion was that the publishers were evidently doing 'their best, and not merely with the blurbs, to turn me into an Irishman' (Beckett, 2009g, 611 n. 1). And, as it happens, he was being presented in that blurb not just as one more Irishman, but as an 'Irish genius'.

Almost a decade earlier, Beckett had opened his first published work – an essay on James Joyce's then 'Work in Progress', published in 1939 under the title *Finnegans Wake* – with a laconic warning: 'The danger is in the neatness of identifications' (Beckett, 1983, 19). That warning bears upon the subsequent sixty years of Beckett's writing life, and it has generally been heeded by commentators on his work, seeking, as they have, for the most part to place the emphasis on failures of identification and the experience of unknowing. And yet, in 1938, Beckett's London publisher was clearly attempting to highlight the author's national identity, and with that a cultural identity as well. In this endeavour, Routledge would prove to be far from alone. For, no matter where one looks, be it in encyclopaedias or the biographical notes often included in editions of his works, among the first things that one learns about Samuel

---

[1] The publishers who rejected *Murphy* included Chatto & Windus (who had published both *Proust* and *More Pricks than Kicks*), Heinemann, Houghton Mifflin, Dent, Cobden-Sanderson, Constable, and Lovat Dickson. Routledge's decision to publish the novel was in part owing to the intervention of Beckett's friend the painter Jack B. Yeats, who recommended it to Routledge in November 1937. As we shall see, Yeats's paintings would come to play a significant role in the articulation of Beckett's views on cultural nationalism.

[2] The poet and art critic Thomas McGreevy (1893–1967) changed the spelling of his surname to MacGreevy in 1943. In the present book, it is spelled MacGreevy throughout.

Beckett is that he was not just a writer, but an *Irish* writer. Today, for instance, the street named after Beckett in Paris's fourteenth arrondissement, in which he lived from 1960 until his death in 1989, identifies him as an '*écrivain irlandais*'. A rare exception to this tendency is the English Heritage blue plaque on 48 Paultons Square, an attractive Georgian terraced house in Chelsea, London, where Beckett lived for seven months, from January to July 1934, before relocating in early August 1934 to a house in Gertrude Street in the same part of London, where he began work on *Murphy* a year later, on 26 August 1935. Unlike the sign in Paris, the plaque in London identifies Beckett simply as a 'Dramatist and Author', with no national ascription. That said, the proximity to his name of the words 'English Heritage' might lead the casual observer to imagine that Beckett was in fact an *English* writer. That impression is only strengthened by the other blue plaque on the same house front, which commemorates the physicist Patrick Blackett. Like Beckett, Blackett was a Nobel Prize winner (in Blackett's case for Physics, in 1948), and he lived in the house in Paultons Square from 1953 to 1969. He was born and died in London.

There is, of course, nothing surprising in the fact that Beckett should have so often been identified as an Irish writer or, as Routledge would have it, an Irish genius. After all, he was born in Ireland, on 13 April 1906, and he would hold Irish citizenship until his death. For all his interest in the experience of ignorance and uncertainty, Beckett's Irish nationality would seem to belong to the kind of facts for which the narrator of his first novel, *Dream of Fair to Middling Women*, calls so stridently: 'Facts, we cannot repeat it too often, let us have facts, plenty of facts' (Beckett, 1992, 74). And yet, in another letter to MacGreevy, written on 31 January 1938, shortly after what would prove to be his permanent remove from Ireland to France in December 1937, Beckett remarked that he suffered from a 'chronic inability to understand as member of any proposition a phrase like "the Irish people"' (Beckett, 2009g, 599). Here, Beckett's philosophical nominalism clearly had political implications. If, for him, the idea of the Irish people was quite simply unintelligible, what could it possibly mean to describe him as a member of that people?

As it happens, Beckett himself reflected on that very question. In May 1964, for instance, in response to an enquiry from the Hungarian publishing house Európa Könyvkiadó, he wrote: 'As a writer I have no national attachment. I am an Irishman (Irish passport) living in France for the past 27 years who has written part of his work in English and part in French' (Beckett, 2014, 601). He was clearly seeking here to distinguish between himself as a politically and legally determined person – technically, an Irish citizen – on the one hand, and as a writer on the other. It was in the latter capacity that he considered himself to have no national attachment. Thus, while it might be legitimate to identify

Beckett as Irish, it would not be justifiable to describe him as an Irish *writer*, since as a writer he accepted no such national affiliation.

The crucial importance of this distinction between Beckett the citizen and Beckett the writer is evident when one turns to the statement that he made in the mid-1950s in his brief homage to the work of his friend the writer and painter Jack B. Yeats (1871–1957). There, Beckett declared laconically that 'The artist who stakes his being is from nowhere, has no kith' (Beckett, 1983, 149). It goes without saying that, for Beckett, the genuine artist, the only one worthy of the name, did indeed stake his or her being, and that therefore no genuine writer's work should ever be considered in terms of any 'national attachment'. To try to make sense of an artist's oeuvre by situating it within a national-cultural context was, for Beckett, utterly misguided, based as it was on a profound misunderstanding of the nature of art.

Beckett's insistence on the separation of the artist from any such national affiliation lay at the heart of his view that art and literature are also completely at odds with any form of cultural nationalism. Art, for him, could never be the expression of the spirit of a particular national culture, any more than the knowledge of a national-cultural context could help to cast light on the meaning of a work of art. Indeed, the artist was, for Beckett, someone who had freed him- or herself from all such national-cultural contexts. Art and cultural nationalism were thus, in his view, two entirely unrelated phenomena. Any form of art that sought to be the expression of a national culture, or to articulate a form of cultural nationalism, was betraying the very idea of art as Beckett understood it. This was a view that he took very early in, and maintained throughout, his writing life. His first-hand experience of the violence and destruction wrought by nationalism across Europe did nothing to weaken his conviction that genuine art is never the expression of, and should never be understood in terms of, a national culture.

What led Beckett to take this position on art's relation (or, more precisely, its non-relation) to national cultures and to cultural nationalism? And what were the implications of that position for his own work? In order to begin to answer those questions, it is first necessary to reflect briefly on the origins of the idea of cultural nationalism against which Beckett was reacting, and the role it had played both in aesthetics and in politics prior to his emergence as a writer in the early 1930s. As we shall see, establishing and then maintaining his detachment from the forces of cultural nationalism was to be far from a simple matter, particularly in an age largely dominated, as Beckett's was, by the ideology of cultural nationalism.

Unlike cosmopolitanism or even patriotism, nationalism is a distinctly modern phenomenon. As Benedict Anderson observes, the age of nationalism began in the eighteenth century, in Western Europe, at a time when religious modes of thought were on the wane. Nationalism offered a new kind of 'imagined community'. The nation was an *imagined* community because its members would never have any personal contact with the vast majority of other members of the nation, although they would feel bound to one another in a collective endeavour. It was also *limited* in the sense that nations were defined in relation to other nations, with no nation conceiving of itself as the nation of humanity as a whole. It was thus intrinsically antagonistic. And it was *sovereign* in the sense that it broke with any 'divinely-ordained, hierarchical dynastic realm' (Anderson, 2016, 6–7). In its origins, nationalism was not necessarily racialist, but it did insist upon a unified culture and a national language.

To place the emphasis squarely upon the manner in which a new ideology of nationalism constituted a break with a dynastic model of communities, however, is to miss the fact that nationalism, and in particular cultural nationalism, was largely a counter-reaction to the cosmopolitan universalism of the French Enlightenment. The great theorists of the nation-state, and the champions of national cultures, were, for the most part, challenging the Enlightenment idea of the human, one that was, to be sure, profoundly Eurocentric and Euro-supremacist, but that appealed to universal values and universal characteristics.

Unlike nationalism, cosmopolitanism was anything but a child of the eighteenth century. Its roots lay in ancient Greece and Rome. It is present in Cicero's *Tusculan Disputations* (c. 45 BCE), for instance, when he quotes the Roman tragedian Marcus Pacuvius (220–130 BCE): 'One's country is wherever one does well' (*Patria est, ubicumque est bene*) (Cicero, 1945, 532–3). Cicero proceeds to remind his readers that, when asked to which country he belonged, Socrates answered: '"To the world," for he regarded himself as a native and citizen of the whole world' (533–5). It was to this ancient conception of the cosmopolitan, confined to and identified with no particular locale, that mid-eighteenth-century writers, above all in France, returned. Among the first writers of the period to engage with the theme was Louis-Charles Fougeret de Monbron (1706–60), in his *The Cosmopolitan, or the Citizen of the World* (1750). Monbron's debt to an ancient idea is evident in his choice of the line from Cicero as his epigraph – *Patria est, ubicumque est bene*. As someone who had travelled widely across Europe, Monbron advocated the cosmopolitan experience as the one best suited to the true understanding of the world. 'The universe is a kind of book', he declared, 'of which one has read only the first page when one has seen only one's own country'. That said, the knowledge to be gleaned from this cosmopolitan life was that all countries were 'almost equally bad' (Monbron, 2010, 1). Ultimately, the lesson of a cosmopolitan lifestyle was that one might as well stay put.

Voltaire's advocacy of cosmopolitanism was considerably less cynical, even if his best-known work today, *Candide* (1759), ends with a conclusion that would have appealed to Monbron. Having suffered in various parts of the world, Candide and his 'little society' settle down on a 'little farm', where they duly cultivate their garden (Voltaire, 2005, 93). The emphasis upon 'little' here stands in clear counterpoint to the sweepingly cosmopolitan adventures that precede this retreat. In fact, Voltaire was among the greatest champions of cosmopolitanism during the Enlightenment, albeit one that was profoundly Eurocentric in nature, to the extent that it might more accurately be termed Europolitanism, and even Western Europolitanism. In a letter written in 1767, for instance, he declared that Europe was becoming a 'great republic of culti-vated minds' (cited in Rougemont, 1966, 148).[3] That republic was transnational and translingual.

In the second half of the eighteenth century, Europe's intellectual elite increasingly saw themselves as inhabiting a space above and beyond any nation-state or particular national culture. In his *Journal of a Tour to the Hebrides* (1785), for instance, Samuel Johnson's biographer, James Boswell, described himself as 'completely a citizen of the world', someone who, in his travels across Europe, 'never felt myself from home' (Boswell, 1958, 6). As for Johnson himself, he is famously recorded in Boswell's *Life of Johnson* (1791) as having considered 'patriotism' to be 'the last refuge of a scoundrel' (Boswell, 1980, 615). Boswell went on to clarify, however, that the patriotism that was being disparaged here was not the kind characterized by a 'real and generous love of our country'; rather, it was 'that pretended patriotism which so many, in all ages and countries, have made a cloak for self-interest' (615). That distinc-tion does not quite have the force to neutralize an apparent contradiction in Johnson's cosmopolitanism, reflected in his view that 'all nations but his own' were 'barbarians' (Boswell, 1958, 6). In addition to highlighting a contradiction at the heart of the cosmopolitan mentality that was far from being limited to Johnson, Boswell's remarks also help to show how the conception of national-ism would evolve out of that of patriotism within the new, late-eighteenth-century context of nation-statism.

Jean-Jacques Rousseau was another major writer of the period to remark upon the disappearance of national characteristics in a new cosmopolitan European space. 'There are', he asserted, 'no more Frenchmen, Germans, Spaniards, even Englishmen, nowadays, regardless of what people may say; there are only Europeans. All have the same tastes, the same passions, the same

---

[3] On Enlightenment cosmopolitanism, see Robertson (2020, ch. 12). On its Eurocentrism, see, for instance, Weller (2021, ch. 2).

morals, because none has been given a national form by a distinctive institution' (Rousseau, 1997, 184). Unlike Voltaire or Boswell, however, Rousseau was far from being an advocate of this absence of national-cultural characteristics. Indeed, in his reflections on the formation of a Polish government, he argued forcefully that Poland should not follow the model of the Western European nations, where there was, in his view, an ever greater 'general European tendency to adopt the tastes and morals of the French', the result being forms of national-cultural degeneration (185).

Rousseau's critique of Enlightenment cosmopolitanism was to exert a considerable influence on German thinkers of the late eighteenth and early nineteenth centuries, among whom Johann Gottfried Herder and Johann Gottlieb Fichte would in due course be particularly influential. Taking their inspiration in part from Rousseau, these counter-French Enlightenment German intellectuals introduced concepts such as the 'spirit of the nation' (*Nationalgeist*), the 'spirit of the people' (*Geist des Volkes*), the 'soul of the people' (*Seele des Volkes*), and the 'genius of the people' (*Genius des Volkes*) into both philosophical and political discourse. In his widely read *Ideas on the Philosophy of the History of Humanity* (1784–91), Herder argued that 'every nation is one people, having its own national form, as well as its own language'. Each nation had what he termed its 'original national character', this being something that could be destroyed and that thus needed to be nurtured and protected (Herder, 1800, 166). According to Herder, the culture produced by each nation was distinguished by this original national character, and no work of art could be understood unless it was considered within the context of that national culture. His long essay on Shakespeare was an attempt to demonstrate precisely this point. The abstract universalism of the French Enlightenment, in which all such national-cultural differences were dissolved, was anathema to Herder, as it was to those German Romantic thinkers who followed in his wake, including the Schlegel brothers. One of the things that they, like Rousseau, had rightly detected in French Enlightenment cosmopolitanism was that beneath its universalist veneer lay a privileging of French culture and the French language. In other words, such cosmopolitanism was, in no small part, a form of French cultural imperialism.

Among the most strident articulations of the emerging cultural nationalism in the wake of the French Revolution and the Napoleonic Wars was that by the German Idealist philosopher Johann Gottlieb Fichte, particularly in his *Addresses to the German Nation*, first delivered as a series of lectures in Berlin from 1804 to 1805, at the height of Napoleon's domination of Continental Europe. In the first of his fourteen addresses to what he identified as the German nation (*die deutsche Nation*), which at that time consisted of a number of separate states, of which Prussia was but one, Fichte declared that 'it is solely by means of the common trait of Germanness that we can avert the downfall of our nation threatened by its confluence with foreign peoples and once more win back a self that is self-supporting and incapable of any form of dependency' (Fichte, 2008, 11). First and foremost, what was required, according to Fichte, was an identification of the distinctive traits of Germanness, and then the establishment of a new German national education to ensure the preservation and cultivation of that Germanness and Germanic culture. Fichte's attempt to define Germanness was pursued by way of a reflection on that which was foreign, both linguistically and culturally. Indeed, for Fichte, the distinction between the Germans and the other peoples of Teutonic descent in Europe was owing above all to the former having remained in the 'original homelands' of the 'ancestral race', as well as their having continued to be native speakers of German, the 'original language' of that race. In contrast, the other Teutonic tribes had migrated, and as a result they had adopted that most contaminating of all cultural forms: a foreign language (Fichte, 2008, 48). The Germanness that Fichte wished to identify, protect, and cultivate was one that found its expression in all cultural forms, not least in art. Consequently, it was possible to determine the value of works of art, including literary works, by assessing the extent to which they conformed to, and expressed, these national-cultural characteristics.

This ideology of cultural nationalism, tied to the idea of national languages, would continue to percolate across Europe throughout the nineteenth century, with its more benign manifestations including the establishment of national galleries, national theatres, and national literary canons. It was an important element in the nationalist movements that resulted in the establishment of major new nation-states in Europe in the second half of the nineteenth century, including Italy in 1861 and Germany in 1871, following the Franco-Prussian War of 1870–1. The founding of the Irish Free State would take another fifty years, being achieved only after the First World War, when Beckett was a teenager.

In the later decades of the nineteenth century, ever more strident forms of nationalism were increasingly shaped by an idea of nationality that extended beyond a shared national language and culture to a shared ethnicity, an element that was already present in the work of both Herder and Fichte. Indeed, the emergence of race theory in the second half of the century led to Europe being increasingly mapped in ethnic terms. Founding publications in this emerging theory of race were the English anatomist and physiologist Robert Knox's *The Races of Men: A Fragment* (1850) and Arthur de Gobineau's influential *Essay on the Inequality of the Human Races* (1853–5). According to Knox, it was possible to distinguish not only between superior and inferior races, but also between the so-called 'European races', those races differing from one another 'as widely as the Negro does from the Bushman' (Knox, 1850, 151). He anticipated a necessary 'war of extermination' against what he variously described as the 'savage', 'inferior', 'dark', and 'depraved' races (162). As for the 'Jewish race', Knox considered it to belong to those 'dark races' against which this war of extermination would need to be waged (300). He thereby established a hierarchical racial mapping that not only distinguished the European from the non-European, but also differentiated hierarchically between racial types within Europe.

It is in this context that one needs to assess the engagement with race theory in the works of thinkers such as Schopenhauer and Nietzsche. It is worth bearing in mind that the Schopenhauer whom Beckett read with such interest in 1930, when preparing his short book on Marcel Proust's *In Search of Lost Time* (1913–27), and whose work he continued to value throughout his life, was the philosopher who could assert that 'The highest civilization and culture, apart from the ancient Hindus and Egyptians, are found exclusively among the white races' (Schopenhauer, 1974, II, 158). This conjunction of nationalism and race theory would culminate in the horror of the Nazi ideology, and ultimately in the death camps, in which some of Beckett's friends and acquaintances would die during the Second World War. Beckett would experience Nazism first hand when he spent six months in Germany from 1936 to 1937, shortly after having completed *Murphy*. It is an experience to which we shall return later in this book.

As noted above, Beckett was a teenager when Ireland secured independence from Britain, following a period of considerable violence on both sides, including the brutal actions of the Black and Tans during the Irish War of Independence (1919–21). Far from putting an end to the violence, the establishment of the Irish Free State in 1922 was followed by the Irish Civil War (1922–3). That Free State, which lasted until December 1937 – as it happens, the month in which Beckett left Ireland to reside permanently in France – was one in which cultural nationalism was particularly prevalent, and one with which Beckett felt no affinity whatsoever. While it is certainly possible to explain this alienation partly in terms of Beckett's coming from a well-to-do Protestant family, it is also important to bear in mind that the writer he valued more than any other – James Joyce – not only came from a Catholic background, but had left Ireland in 1904, never to return, and that his novel *Ulysses* (1922) had been banned in Ireland. In other words, the Irish cultural nationalism in which Beckett grew up was one that excluded the art that he revered the most. Any reflection upon Beckett's Protestantism needs to remain mindful of his unstinting appreciation of Joyce's work and, indeed, of Joyce's life of exile, in which, like his hero Stephen Dedalus, he sought to escape the 'nets' not only of language and religion, but also of 'nationality' (Joyce, 1991, 254).

Beckett's resistance to cultural nationalism was apparent from the outset of his writing life, and certainly before his visit to Nazi Germany. And it was far from being incidental. Indeed, as we shall see, it was present in much of his work, taking different forms in different periods. It was never, however, simply a matter of rejecting cultural nationalism in favour of some form of abstract universalism. Things were to prove to be far more complicated than that. It would be a mistake to assume, for instance, that Beckett became a cosmopolitan writer, comfortably inhabiting a European republic of letters of the kind to which Voltaire referred. In certain key respects, Beckett was closer to Monbron. Having travelled across Europe, including visits to London, Constantinople, Rome, Naples, Venice, Florence, Berlin, Dresden, Barcelona, and Madrid, Monbron came to realize not only that he was completely indifferent to where he resided, as long as he was free, but that the cosmopolitan experience was in fact a nihilistic one. As he scathingly put it: 'I confess in all good faith that I am worth precisely nothing, and that the only difference there is between others and myself is that I am bold enough to take off the mask' (Monbron, 2010, 16).

Moreover, while the cosmopolitan believes that, as Boswell put it, s/he belongs everywhere, Beckett's work testifies increasingly to the experience of those who feel themselves to belong nowhere. Beckett's figures are far closer in spirit to medieval Christians such as the twelfth-century Saxon canon Hugh of Saint Victor (c. 1096–1141), who considered the true mode of being to be a fundamental homelessness. As Hugh of Saint Victor put it in his *Didascalicon*: 'The man who finds his homeland sweet is still a tender beginner; he to whom every soil is as his native land is already strong; but he is perfect to whom the entire world is as a foreign land' (Saint Victor, 1991, 101). Beckett's resistance to cultural nationalism would lead him not to cosmopolitanism, but towards an experience of foreignness, although not one grounded in the Christian belief in a spiritual home, even if he often resorted to Christian motifs and images, these remaining in place even when almost all other markers of cultural affiliation had been stripped away.

The following three sections chart Beckett's various attempts to break free from any national-cultural context, to escape above all the net of cultural nationalism, and to explore the experience of being what might be termed a citizen of nowhere – or, to take up a term from Joyce's *Finnegans Wake*, an uneasy inhabitant of 'Noland' (see Ellmann, 1987, 103–4). Section 2 focuses on Beckett's struggle against cultural nationalism in his English-language works between 1929 and 1945. Section 3 turns to his major works in French between

1946 and the late 1950s, where he undertook an extraordinary disorientation of cultural references, in part through his (often painful) work of self-translation. Section 4 explores his later works of prose and drama, in which it is ever less possible to locate human beings in relation to anything that might be termed a nation-state or a national culture, even though the Christian motifs remain. This late vision of the human is neither national nor cosmopolitan. Rather, it offers a new way of imagining the human, one in which the distinctions between nations and cultures break down, and in which one can glimpse another way of being. It is far from a reassuring vision, but it is one that challenges us to question some of our most fundamental assumptions about imagined communities, and about possible ways of being and belonging.

2 A Nameless and Hideous Mass

Beckett's resistance to cultural nationalism is evident even in his earliest literary efforts. In certain respects, his first substantial literary work, the posthumously published novel *Dream of Fair to Middling Women* (written in 1931–2), is a profoundly cosmopolitan work. Those cosmopolitan credentials are evident not least in the setting, which ranges across a number of European capitals, from Dublin to Paris to Vienna. In its language and range of literary references, too, *Dream* seems to insist upon its cultural cosmopolitanism. Latin, French, German, and Italian phrases pepper its English, while Continental European writers and thinkers dominate the novel's cultural landscape. These range from the Ancient Greek and Roman (Homer, Virgil, Horace, Sallust) to French (Ronsard, Malherbe, Racine, Sade, Chenier, Stendhal, Vigny, Balzac, Musset, Rimbaud, Mallarmé, Gide, Proust), German and Austrian (Hölderlin, Schopenhauer, Nietzsche, Sacher-Masoch, Freud), Italian (Dante, Leopardi, D'Annunzio), Russian (Pushkin, Dostoevsky), and Spanish (José Ignacio de Espronceda y Delgado). There are also references to numerous English writers, including Marlowe, Shakespeare, Byron, Austen, and Dickens. Far less frequent are the references to writers of Irish extraction. The nods to European painting and music are just as cosmopolitan, including the artists Botticelli, Bosch, Dürer, Rembrandt, El Greco, Watteau, Blake, and Cézanne, and the composers Mozart, Beethoven, Chopin, Brahms, and Wagner. As for the novel's protagonist, his name, Belacqua, shorn of any family name, is taken from Dante's *Purgatorio*, and could scarcely be less Irish.

While all of the above might seem to suggest a decidedly Eurocentric cosmopolitanism, Beckett was careful to counter this impression through the inclusion of references to the Persian poets Saadi and Hafez, and, more importantly, a number of references to Chinese culture. There is, for instance, the 'little story about China'; that is, the tale of Lîng-Lûin, who 'went to the confines of the West' (Beckett, 1992, 10). This was derived from Louis Laloy's book *La Musique chinoise* (c. 1910).[4] And then there is the anecdote concerning the Chinese Empress Wu (111), taken from H. A. Giles's *The Civilisation of China* (1910).[5] By the time Beckett came to write *Dream*, an interest in Chinese culture had already been established as a feature of Anglophone modernism, above all by Ezra Pound, whose translations of classical Chinese poetry had been published in 1915 under the title *Cathay*.

For a writer who, as we shall see, would go on to disorientate and then strip away almost all national-cultural references, the opening of *Dream* could not be more nationally situated. As Seán Kennedy observes, Beckett's engagement with the idea of the nation, and in particular his inclusion of signs of national belonging, was far from being constant across the sixty years of his writing life (see Kennedy, 2010, 10–11). There is, rather, a clear trajectory, albeit one that is neither simple nor uninterruptedly monodirectional. In *Dream*, the reader first encounters Belacqua sitting on the stanchion of 'Carlyle Pier' (Beckett, 1992, 3). It is taken for granted that readers will know to which pier Beckett is referring here, and thus that they are familiar with Dublin and its environs. The pier in question is Carlisle Pier in Dún Laoghaire harbour. Constructed between 1853 and 1855, it took its name from Frederick Howard, fifth Earl of Carlisle (1748–1825) and Lord Lieutenant of Ireland. This pier was the place from which generations of Irish emigrants would depart, seeking a better life abroad (principally in England, Australia, New Zealand, and the United States) than the one available to them in an Ireland ruled from London. In other words, the foreign-named Belacqua is located from the outset within a context that is culturally and nationally conflicted, evoking as it does the tensions and hardships of a long history of often brutal colonial rule, followed by a decade of Irish independence in which a Catholic-leaning cultural nationalism was increasingly dominant.

Beckett's protagonist is clearly deemed not to belong there. While, to those readers familiar with Dante's *Purgatorio*, his name evokes stasis, it is from the outset movement that is required of Belacqua. A wharfinger is soon instructing him to 'Get off my pier' (Beckett, 1992, 7). That historically charged landmark is not a place that Belacqua can comfortably inhabit. It does not belong to him, and he does not belong there. And this is something that he accepts without a fight: 'It even seemed natural enough to Belacqua that the man should speak of the pier as his' (7). The novel's opening scene ends with a trope that will become central to Beckett's oeuvre: an expulsion. Having been ordered to leave the pier,

---

[4] See Pilling (2004, 35).   [5] See ibid. (205).

Belacqua 'had no choice but to hobble away on his ruined feet' (8). In short, the opening pages of Beckett's first novel suggest that Ireland is no genuine home for his protagonist. His sense of unbelonging is at least as political and cultural as it is philosophical.

Notwithstanding the various ways in which *Dream* presents itself as a cosmopolitan work, that opening scene already points elsewhere: to an experience of being at home nowhere rather than everywhere. And this impression is only strengthened when we learn that, for all his travels across Continental Europe, what Belacqua seeks is neither a national-cultural home in Ireland nor a home in some cosmopolitan sphere, but rather a placeless place, without history, locatable on no geopolitical map. As Beckett puts it: 'The chase to Vienna, the flight to Paris, the slouch to Fulda, the relapse into Dublin and . . . immunity like hell from journeys and cities' (Beckett, 1992, 120). At home neither in Dublin nor in any of the Continental capitals, Belacqua withdraws into the 'wombtomb' (45). While that purely mental space is characterized, as has often been noted, by the negation of the 'mistral of desire', as well as of the understanding, it is also an 'asylum' in another, political and cultural sense (44), for it is stripped of all national-cultural signifiers. It is, in short, neither a national nor an international-cosmopolitan space.

This flight from the world can, however, only be a temporary one, and finding a language in which to capture it proves challenging. As noted above, Beckett scatters large doses of French and German, as well as bits of Latin and Italian, across his first novel, demanding a level of multilingualism of the reader that militates against national-cultural limitations. The demands that he places upon his readers are such that only the highly literate cosmopolitan is likely to be able to make much sense of the text. Indeed, Beckett strains for an ever wider linguistic range, beyond even his own prodigious gifts. At one point, for instance, his narrator asks: 'what's the Dutch for randy', flagging a lacuna in his multilingual word hoard (Beckett, 1992, 72). At the same time, it is in *Dream* that, unlike Joyce, who was then seeking to create his own unique language (beyond the 'nets' of Irish and standard English) in what would become *Finnegans Wake*, Beckett first expresses the idea that French might be the language best suited to his work. As he has Belacqua declare when reflecting on how to write 'without style': 'Perhaps only the French language can give you the thing you want' (48).

This conception of a writing that is without style constitutes an important departure from Beckett's Joycean conception of language in his 1929 essay, 'Dante . . . Bruno . Vico .. Joyce' (1929). There, he had argued approvingly that the language of Joyce's 'Work in Progress' was anything but lacking in style. As he put it: 'Here is the savage economy of hieroglyphics. Here words are not the polite contortions of 20th century printer's ink. They are alive. They elbow their way on to the page, and glow and blaze and fade and disappear' (Beckett, 1983, 28). This living language stands in stark opposition to standard English, which, Beckett asserts, is 'abstracted to death' (28). As it happens, this conception of a particular kind of language as sensuously 'alive' bears a striking similarity to Fichte's nationalist idea of German as a 'living language' in his *Addresses to the German Nation* of 1804–5. There, Fichte had insisted on a fundamental distinction between German and the 'neo-Latin languages' (Fichte, 2008, 58) – the equivalent of the English language in Beckett's essay on Joyce. According to Fichte, those among the Teutonic tribes who continued to speak the 'original language of the ancestral race' spoke a language that had 'developed continuously out of the actual life of the nation' (60). For native speakers of German, the relation between culture and life, spirit and action, remained organic and alive, in contrast to the dead signs employed by those who had taken up a foreign (neo-Latin) language. In short, German was a 'living' language in the way that Europe's Romance languages were not (61). As Fichte put it, anticipating Beckett on Joyce:

> In a living language the sign itself is immediately alive and sensuous, representing anew the whole of its own life and thus taking hold of the same and intervening in it. To the possessor of such a language the spirit speaks directly, and reveals itself to him as one man to another. By contrast, the sign of the dead language does not immediately stimulate anything. (63)

Beckett's shift towards the idea of a French language 'without style' in *Dream* is thus a significant step away not only from the position he had taken only a few years earlier, but also from a Fichtean culturally nationalist conception of language.

That said, Beckett's privileging of French has its own important place in the history of the struggle between nationalist and cosmopolitan tendencies in Europe, and does not constitute anything like a clean break with cultural-nationalist conceptions of language. During the Enlightenment, for all their apparent universalism, French cosmopolitans almost always privileged French culture and the French language over all others. This national-cultural underbelly to ostensible universalism was something that German thinkers in particular took pleasure in exposing, as they sought to promote Germanic culture. Herder's loathing of all things French was undoubtedly in part a rejection of a form of cultural supremacism dressed up as universalism.

The privileging of the French language was nowhere more in evidence than in a work published in 1784 under the title *Discourse on the Universality of the French Language,* by the journalist Antoine de Rivarol (1753–1801). Like

Voltaire, Rivarol considered eighteenth-century Europe to have become an 'immense republic' (Rivarol, 2013, 48). And, in his view, this European republic now required a shared language. That language should, he maintained, be French, on account of its 'admirable clarity' and the high quality of its literature. As he put it: 'That which is not clear is not French; that which is not clear is still English, Italian, Greek, or Latin' (90). He considered the French language, with its 'natural' syntactical logic of subject, verb, object, to incarnate the very essence of Enlightenment universality. Rivarol's assumption that a transnational republic should have a shared language, rather than being a multilingual space, was itself a sign of how the nationalist and the cosmopolitan visions were far from being simply diametrically opposed.

The privileging of French in *Dream of Fair to Middling Women* belongs to this long tradition of considering French to be the cosmopolitan language par excellence. Again, however, Beckett is here gesturing towards the cosmopolitan only in due course to take his readers elsewhere, for the French of Beckett's post-war work would prove to be not the language of those who belong everywhere (in the true cosmopolitan spirit) but rather the language of those who belong nowhere. Such a writing without style is, as has often been observed, an impoverished language, in which there are far fewer linguistic fireworks of the kind one finds throughout the, at times, barely readable *Dream*. In Beckett's post-war works in French, first evident in *Mercier and Camier*, the four novellas, and *Molloy*, this writing without style will also prove to be a language in which national-cultural signifiers play a disorientating role, frustrating any clear national-cultural identifications, without simply lifting the reader into some abstract universalism. This suggests, as we shall see, that Beckett recognized, as writers such as Voltaire and Rivarol did not, that beneath any apparent cosmopolitanism there is almost always national-cultural bias.

Just as he would not begin to achieve such a writing 'without style' until after the Second World War, and following his switch to French, so, in *Dream*, Beckett makes no effort to avoid national-cultural signifiers. Like his early poems, some of which would be included in the collection *Echo's Bones and Other Precipitates* (1935), his first novel teems with references to its Irish setting, and in particular to Dublin and its environs, from Carlisle Pier to O'Connell Bridge, from Chapelizod to Kilmainham. In many respects, it is as rooted in the world of Dublin as are the stories in Joyce's *Dubliners* (1914). While, as his narrator insists, there may be 'no real Belacqua' (Beckett, 1992, 121), that unreal figure is located within an all too real Irish setting. For all his travels across Europe, for all the languages on display, for all the myriad cultural references, the novel begins and ends in Ireland. And that Ireland is explicitly identified as 'home'. The penultimate section of the novel, for instance (entitled

'Three'), opens with Belacqua's return from Continental Europe being characterized precisely as a journey home: 'They took the coast road home, three days and three nights they dawdled up homeward along it, by Youghal, Tramore, Wicklow Town, living on the fat of the land' (143). And the novel's short epilogue (entitled 'And') clearly evokes the end of Joyce's *Dubliners*. In place of the latter's 'faintly falling' snow, which unifies all those on the island of Ireland, both the living and the dead, Beckett opts for rain, which falls in *Dream* with 'a rather desolate uniformity' upon 'the bay, the champaign-land and the mountains, and notably upon the central bog' (239; cf. Joyce, 2000a, 225). That rain, Beckett writes, is part of Ireland's 'charm'. The unity it brings is, however, even more desolate than that of Joyce's snow, not least because rain is a lot more common in Ireland than is snow.

While Beckett's first novel may open and close in an Ireland identified as home, it is one that proves to be no genuine homeland for Belacqua. He does not see himself as belonging there, and he does not identify with the culture or the nation. Rather, he wishes to be elsewhere, 'no matter where, anywhere, anywhere bar Moscow and England' (Beckett, 1992, 176). Ironically, far from shunning Moscow, Beckett wrote to the film-maker Sergei Eisenstein in the mid-1930s, offering to come to Russia to work for him. And as for England, it was in the latter that Beckett would seek to establish himself as a writer in the mid-1930s, following his failure to secure a publisher for *Dream*. His first books – a monograph on *Proust* (1931) and a collection of short stories partly derived from *Dream*, and published under the title *More Pricks Than Kicks* (1934) – were both published by the London house of Chatto & Windus.

If the stories in *More Pricks Than Kicks* constitute a step back from the structural and stylistic innovations of *Dream*, they also mark a retreat from the apparent cosmopolitanism of his first novel – 'apparent' because, as we have seen, it is, in fact, a withdrawal from both the national and the international that Belacqua seeks to achieve. As Andrew Gibson observes, the Belacqua of *More Pricks Than Kicks* is 'both inclined and disinclined to shrug off the culture from which he stems' (Gibson, 2010, 38). The range of Continental European cultural references is far more limited in *More Pricks Than Kicks*, and the setting is more consistently Irish. In this, the volume bears even more of a resemblance to Joyce's *Dubliners*, although with the focus falling upon a single Dubliner, who has now acquired a surname, the Belacqua of *Dream* having become Belacqua Shuah. That said, the opening story, 'Dante and the Lobster', locates Belacqua not in Ireland (as in *Dream*) but in a foreign literary work, Dante's *Paradiso*. And, in the second story, 'Fingal', Belacqua's gaze is focused not on Fingal but rather on France. He compares the Fingal landscape to Saône-et-Loire, the latter being 'a champaign land for the sad and serious, not a bloody little toy Kindergarten like Wicklow' (Beckett, 2010d, 18). In the penultimate story, 'Yellow', in which Belacqua dies during a routine operation on account of an error by one of the Irish medical staff, Beckett provides an insight into why Belacqua should feel so alienated from this Irish world in which he finds himself. He is, we learn, a 'dirty low-down Low Church Protestant high-brow' (163). As numerous commentators have observed, any assessment of Beckett's own sense of not feeling at home in the Irish Free State, and his engagement with this sense of non-belonging in his fiction, has to take account of his sense of Ireland as divided along religious lines, with all the cultural implications of that division.

For all his sense of alienation from it, there can be no doubt that Beckett took a considerable interest in Irish culture. As Alan Graham observes, this is evidenced not least by the 'Trueborn Jackeen' notes, dating from the 1930s (see Graham, 2015).[6] The title 'Trueborn Jackeen' alludes to Daniel Defoe's satirical poem *The True-Born Englishman* (1701). In that poem, Defoe defended the Dutch-born King William III (William of Orange) against xeno-phobic attacks by his political enemies, and ridiculed the idea of English racial purity. The 'true-born Englishman' proves to derive from 'a Mixture of all Kinds' and to be an 'Het'rogeneous *Thing*' (Defoe, 1997). While nothing came of his 'Trueborn Jackeen' project, Beckett's notes nonetheless testify to an interest in reworking Defoe's satire as an attack on notions of Irish racial, linguistic, and cultural purity.

Beckett's highly critical attitude towards Catholic Ireland in the 1930s is captured with particular venom in the essay that he wrote in 1935 on Irish censorship. In 'Censorship in the Saorstat',[7] another work for which he was unable to find a publisher, he highlighted the Irish prohibition of works advo-cating the use of contraceptives, again contrasting Ireland with France, and sarcastically noting that while 'France may commit race suicide, Erin never will' (Beckett, 1983, 86). Ireland had, in his view, become a nation-state that prioritized population growth over intellectual development, or, as he put it, 'Sterilization of the mind and apotheosis of the litter' (87). As we shall see, the animalization of the Irish suggested by the word 'litter' here recurs in Beckett's own fiction during the Second World War, in a far more disturbing context.

A year before writing this essay on censorship, in a review of recent Irish poetry, Beckett had already made his views abundantly clear on literary works

---

[6] Trinity College Dublin (TCD) MS 10971/2/8. On these notes and their relevance to *Molloy*, see also O'Reilly, Van Hulle, and Verhulst (2017, 289).

[7] The Saorstat was the Irish Free State (*Saorstát Éireann*). In *Murphy*, the alternative to the political 'free state' is the freedom achieved by complete withdrawal into the mind, as a counter-space to the political. This latter freedom proves, however, to be fatal.

that sought to engage with and champion Irish national culture. Those writers who belonged to the Irish Literary Revival – the so-called Celtic Twilight – in the later nineteenth and early twentieth centuries were, in his view, to be dismissed as 'antiquarians' (Beckett, 1983, 70). The taking up of what was seen as an authentic Gaelic heritage, within an Irish nationalist movement, was completely anathema to Beckett's conception of the artist. That Gaelic heritage – in the form of the medieval Ulster and Fenian cycles – was, he asserted, no more than 'cut-and-dried sanctity and loveliness' (71). Those 'younger antiquarians' whose poetry was to be dismissed as aesthetically worthless, in no small part because it sought its material in that Irish national culture, included Oliver St John Gogarty (1878–1957), James Stephens (1880–1950), Austin Clarke (1896–1974), Frederick Robert Higgins (1896–1941, who, like Beckett, had been born in Foxrock), Monk Gibbon (1896–1987), and Brian O'Higgins (1882–1963). As for the greatest of the writers associated with the Celtic Twilight, William Butler Yeats (1865–1939), he had finally come to recognize that all those 'old mythologies' should be discarded. As he put it in the poem 'A Coat', in *Responsibilities* (1914), there was 'more enterprise / In walking naked' (Yeats, 1989, 127). In this, Yeats would prove to be a model for Beckett.

As for the few Irish writers whom Beckett considered to possess any artistic merit, it was precisely in their rejection of the Irish national-cultural heritage that they distinguished themselves. Among these, the poet for whom Beckett had the warmest praise was not Yeats, but rather his own friend Denis Devlin (1908–59), whose volume *Intercessions* would be published in 1937 by the Europa Press, which two years earlier had published Beckett's collection *Echo's Bones and Other Precipitates*. The value of Devlin's poetry lay, according to Beckett, in no small part in its breaking with the tradition represented by 'the Gossoon's Wunderhorn of that Irish Romantic Arnim-Brentano combination, Sir Samuel Ferguson and Standish O'Grady' (Beckett, 1983, 76). Ferguson (1810–86) and O'Grady (1846–1928) were two of the principal figures in the Irish Revival, the latter even being known as 'the Father of the Irish Literary Revival', which coincided with national-cultural movements across Europe, not least in the German Reich that was established after Prussia's victory in the Franco-Prussian War of 1870–1. The connection that he saw between Irish and German cultural nationalism was made very clear by Beckett here, through his allusion to the collection of German folk songs *The Boy's Magic Horn*, edited by Achim von Arnim and Clemens Brentano, and first published in three editions between 1805 and 1808, at the very time that Fichte was delivering his *Addresses to the German Nation*. It is worth bearing in mind that when, in August 1934, Beckett wrote his essay on 'Recent Irish Poetry', in which he dismissed Irish cultural nationalism and compared it to the equivalent movement in Germany, the Nazi Party was already in power there. His repeated contrasting of Ireland and France in the early 1930s was thus complemented by the suggestion that Irish and German nationalism were very similar. This gives a clear sense of just how polemical Beckett's engagement with the issue of cultural nationalism was in the 1930s. He was quite prepared to elide profound differences in prosecuting his anti-nationalist agenda.

While Beckett's focus in his review of recent Irish poetry on the seemingly more abstract philosophical experience of what he termed a 'rupture of the lines of communication' between the subject and the object, mind and world (Beckett, 1983, 70), might lead one to think that his aesthetics did not have a political dimension, nothing could be further from the truth. That insistence upon a rupture between mind and world was nothing less than a call for art to stand as a counter to cultural nationalism. Like Belacqua's 'wombtomb', this experience of a breakdown in the relation between mind and world was in no small part a liberation of the mind from any national-cultural context, and, as we shall see, also from any cosmopolitan-international alternative.

Now living in London, it was also in 1935 that Beckett began work on his second novel – the first to find a publisher. Like *Dream*, *Murphy* (1938) begins by locating its protagonist in a particular national-cultural context. Whereas Belacqua is first encountered on Carlisle Pier in Dún Laoghaire, Murphy is living in a mews house in West Brompton, London. Just as *Dream* opposes Ireland to Continental Europe, so *Murphy* is also in many respects a bipolar novel, not simply because at its heart lies the opposition between mind and world (as explored in chapter 6 of the novel), but also because its two worlds are those of London and Dublin. Neither of these proves to be a home to Murphy, but it is the latter that comes in for the most mockery. Murphy has fled to London from Ireland, seeking to detach himself from that world. He is pursued, however, by various representatives of that world on account of the Irish Miss Counihan's desire for him. To escape the Irish cultural net proves to be anything but straightforward.

The novel includes numerous humorous attacks on Irish cultural nationalism. There is, for instance, the scene in which Mr Neary bangs his head against the buttocks of the statue of Cuchulain in the General Post Office in Dublin, Cuchulain being the most celebrated of all Irish mythological figures (Beckett, 2009i, 29). As for the woman who desires Murphy: 'For an Irish girl Miss Counihan was', the reader is informed, 'quite exceptionally anthropoid' (75). And then, doubling down on his criticism of Irish poets in his 1934 review, Beckett lampoons the poet Austin Clarke in the figure of the 'pot poet' Austin Ticklepenny, from the county of Dublin (55). Clarke, whose reputation at the time was second only to that of W. B. Yeats in Ireland, recognized himself as the object of mockery and was inclined to take legal action against Beckett.

Liberating oneself from one's national-cultural origins is, however, no easy matter, as *Murphy* testifies. Among the many failures depicted in the novel, one of the most significant is Murphy's inability to free himself from the hold of that Irish national culture. Indeed, even death proves insufficient. Unlike Belacqua, Murphy is, of course, very obviously a name associated with Ireland, to the point of it even being used as a denigrating common noun for the Irish. And, as Neary observes to Murphy's English landlady, Miss Carridge: 'we have torn ourselves from the groves of Blarney, for the sole purpose of cajoling him in private' (140). And then there is Murphy's birthmark, located on one of his buttocks, this mocking of the Irish national-cultural identification echoing the scene in which Neary embraces Cuchulain's buttocks. The importance of this birthmark is evident in its remaining visible despite the fire that is the cause of Murphy's death. In the morgue, Neary identifies Murphy to the coroner as a 'native of the city of Dublin', to which the coroner responds: 'Dear old indelible Dublin' (166). Just as *Dream* ends with an evocation of Joyce's *Dubliners*, Beckett's rain replacing Joyce's snow, so this scene in the morgue also evokes Joyce, the phrase 'dirty old Dublin' appearing in *Dubliners*, *Ulysses*, and *Finnegans Wake*, where it becomes 'teary turty Taubling' (Joyce, 2000b, 7). Significantly, the modifier added by Beckett here is 'indelible'. It is in that word that the challenge of escaping from the Irish national-culture net becomes clear. Joyce's Stephen Dedalus declares that he will have to rely on 'cunning' and 'silence' to escape those nets. As we shall see, Beckett will pursue a different course, first by way of the French language and then through the disorientations of a bilingual oeuvre. The bipolarity of *Murphy* is a step in that direction.

Following the completion of *Murphy* in June 1936, Beckett's views on cultural nationalism were sharpened considerably by his six-month stay in Nazi Germany, from October 1936 to March 1937, when he travelled across the country to view public and private art collections, with halts in various cultural centres, including Hamburg, Berlin, Weimar, Leipzig, Dresden, and Munich. Notwithstanding the obvious risks, Beckett's letters from Germany during that time included a number of stinging remarks that reveal his attitude towards the Nazi regime's rabid cultural nationalism. On 28 November 1936, for instance, in a letter to Thomas MacGreevy, whom he had identified as an 'independent' in his 1934 review of recent Irish poetry (Beckett, 1983, 74), he observed that 'living art' was only to be found in private art collections in Germany, now that most galleries had been purged, and that the Nazi campaign against 'Art-Bolshevism' was 'only just beginning' (Beckett, 2009g, 387).

Among the major differences between his earlier experience of a religiously inflected cultural nationalism in Ireland and the cultural nationalism in Nazi Germany was the racial dimension in the latter. His recognition of this is apparent in various letters, including the one to MacGreevy cited above, in which Beckett referred to his encounter with a 'Proust fiend' who was working on a doctoral thesis on the French novelist, observing that 'there is something magnificent in doing a doctorate in 1936 with a work on not merely an "exquisite", but a non-Aryan' (Beckett, 2009g, 389). From Munich, he wrote to MacGreevy on 7 March 1937 that Nuremberg was now 'the industrial centre of Bavaria and with Munich & Berlin the third centre of Nazidiffusion and the seat of Jewbaiting Streicher & his rag' (461). The newspaper in question was *Der Stürmer*, the anti-Semitic tabloid founded by Julius Streicher in 1923, which enjoyed a circulation of almost half a million at the time of Beckett's letter. Beckett's loathing of nationalism was at its most evident, however, in a diary entry on 15 January 1937, in which he noted of the expressions 'historical necessity' and 'Germanic destiny' that they 'start the vomit moving upwards' (cited in Nixon, 2011, 87). While in Germany, he read the nationalist book *Deutschlands Leben* (1930) by Hans Pferdmenges, only to dismiss it in his diary as 'NS Kimmwasser', or Nazi bilge.

On his return from Germany, Beckett's anti-nationalism was redirected against its original object, Ireland, albeit inflected now with some choice German terms picked up on his travels. On 28 September 1937, for instance, he wrote to MacGreevy: 'There is no animal I loathe more profoundly than a Civic Guard, a symbol of Ireland with his official Gaelic loutish complacency & pot-walloping Schreinlichkeit'. As the editors of Beckett's correspondence observe, *Schreinlichkeit* is a portmanteau word meaning 'chest-ishness' (Beckett, 2009g, 555 n. 5). In another letter to MacGreevy, dated 31 January 1938 and thus following what would prove to be his permanent move to Paris, Beckett stated that he considered the writer and painter Jack B. Yeats, the brother of W. B. Yeats, to have turned decisively 'away from the local'. It was in this same letter that he confessed to his own 'chronic inability to understand as member of any proposition a phrase like "the Irish people"' (599).

In the months following his relocation to Paris at the end of 1937, Beckett's attitude towards the idea of the Irish people grew only more extreme, and it is clear that he again detected similarities between Irish and German nationalism. In a letter to MacGreevy on 31 January 1938, for instance, he declared that he could only imagine the 'Irish people' as 'a nameless and hideous mass' (Beckett, 2009g, 600). This was a comment with a considerable bearing upon his view of his friend's own work. He had championed MacGreevy's poetry in his 1934 review of recent Irish poetry, where he described it as 'shining and intensely personal verse'.[8] Four years later, he was prepared to acknowledge that he did not appreciate MacGreevy's cultural-nationalist turn. As he put it: 'I, as a clot of prejudices, prefer the first half of your work, with its real and radiant individuals, to the second, with our national scene' (600). This remark is of a piece with Beckett's politically nominalist preference for the individual over the collective.

The months following his remove to Paris were a period when Beckett was clearly signalling his intention to detach himself from Ireland not only geographically and culturally, but also linguistically. In a letter dated 3 April 1938, for instance, he informed MacGreevy: 'I have the feeling that any poems there may happen to be in the future will be in French' (Beckett, 2009g, 614). This turn to French coincided with an ongoing sensitivity to forms of aggressive cultural nationalism, and may thus be seen in that political light. In a letter to his literary agent George Reavey from Paris on 27 September 1938, for instance, he mentioned having heard 'Adolf the Peacemaker' on the radio, and having thought that he was listening to the sound of 'air escaping – a slow puncture' (642). Six months later, on 18 April 1939, with war looming, he wrote to MacGreevy from Paris, informing him that 'If there is a war, as I fear there must be soon, I shall place myself at the disposition of this country' (656). What had become clear to Beckett by that fateful year in the history of Europe was that his allegiances now lay not only with the French rather than the English language, but politically with France rather than Ireland, to the point of his being prepared to sacrifice his life in the defence of his adopted country. Ireland's neutrality during the Second World War was not something that he could endorse. Following the German defeat of France in 1940, he joined a French Resistance group and thereby put his life in jeopardy for a political cause. Before long, he was having to flee south to avoid arrest and, at best, imprisonment in a German concentration camp, after the Resistance cell to which he belonged was exposed.

While committing himself to France in face of the Nazi aggressor, and despite his tentative experiments in French at the end of the 1930s, when in 1941 he eventually started work on his next novel, *Watt*, Beckett returned to the English language and to a recognizably Irish setting. Much of this work, his last novel in English, was written in Roussillon in the unoccupied South of France, in the so-called Vichy regime led by Marshal Philippe Pétain. Beckett would later describe the novel as an escape from the horrors through which much of Continental Europe was then passing, under the yoke of Nazi tyranny. Many

---

[8] This review was published under the title 'Humanistic Quietism' in the *Dublin Magazine* (July–September 1934). The theme of humanism would recur in Beckett's review of MacGreevy's book on Yeats, although this time in relation to questions of cultural nationalism.

years later, on receiving a book of photographs of the Warsaw Ghetto taken by a German soldier in 1941, Beckett would thank the sender for his work on 'that hellish place at that hellish time' (Beckett, 2016, 639). There can be no doubt that he was preoccupied by the progress of the war, and that he would later be acutely aware of the appalling suffering inflicted on so many by German nationalism.

As has often been noted, however, among the many striking features of *Watt* is the fact that, while written in France during the war, not only is it set in a world resembling the one in which Beckett grew up, while playing on the genre of the Irish Protestant 'big house' novel, but it also excludes any allusions to the war that was raging in Europe during the entire period of its composition (1941–5). In that sense, it did indeed constitute something of a refuge from contemporary history. That is not to say, however, that in *Watt* Beckett abandoned his engagement with matters political, and in particular with the issue of cultural nationalism. Far from it.

In many respects, *Watt* is a decidedly transitional work, taking the reader from a recognizably Irish world to one that is ever less locatable, ever more abstracted. The novel opens with a scene that, like the opening of *Dream*, plays on the issue of possession. While, as we have seen, the Belacqua of *Dream* acknowledges that the pier is not 'his', and thus moves on, *Watt* opens with Mr Hackett seeing what he considers to be 'his seat' (Beckett, 2009j, 3). Here, though, there is no nationally identified place, no proper name to situate the scene. Possession, and the role of the state therein, nonetheless remains central here. For the narrator observes that, notwithstanding the fact that Mr Hackett 'thought of it as his', the seat in question was 'the property very likely of the municipality, or of the public' (3). An even more overt politicization of seating follows soon thereafter, when, in conversation with a woman named Tetty, Mr Hackett refers to his father 'breaking stones on Prince William's Seat' (10), this being the highest peak in Ireland, located on the border of the Wicklow and Dublin Mountains, and the sight of a stone quarry. This 'seat' was probably named after the brother of King George IV, following a royal visit to Ireland in 1821.

As for the eponymous protagonist, when he eventually appears, Watt does so not as a person, but as an 'it', a 'solitary figure' that cannot be clearly distinguished from a parcel, a carpet, or a role of tarpaulin (11). When quizzed as to Watt's 'nationality, family, birthplace, confession, occupation, means of existence, distinctive signs' – such as a birthmark of the kind that enabled the national-cultural identification of Murphy's corpse – Mr Nixon declares not only that he personally knows nothing, but that 'nothing is known' (16). This is the appearance of a new kind of figure in Beckett's work, one that is wholly detached from any national affiliation. Watt may be situated in a distinctly Irish environ, but he himself does not belong to it. And this detachment from the national is far from being restricted to Watt, for the world of this novel is one in which those national-cultural markers that are still operative in Beckett's earlier work begin to break down. In his decidedly long 'short statement', for instance, Arsene, remarking on the expression 'six of one and half a dozen of the other', cannot be sure whether it is English or Irish: 'do I confuse them [the English] with the Irish?', he asks himself, before abandoning the issue (49).

The desire for national-cultural identifiers is itself subject to mockery here. In the 'incident of the Galls', for instance, when Watt is so troubled by the fact that 'nothing had happened, with all the clarity and solidity of something' (63), his inability to accept this experience leads the narrator (later identified as Sam) to ask: 'One wonders sometimes where Watt thought he was. In a culture park?' (63). This cultural disorientation, when the very distinction between the Irish and its salient other starts to break down, enacts the dissolution of the concept of the 'Irish people' to which Beckett had objected to strenuously in his correspondence with MacGreevy. It does not, however, entirely rein in his impulse to mock Irish culture – and, more precisely, Irish Catholic culture – in his big (Protestant) house novel. The clearest example of this is the story of the Lynch family, in which he again ridicules the Catholic attitude to contraception (84ff). The extremely large Lynch family, including a mother with over twenty children, which results from the rejection on religious grounds of any form of contraception, is characterized by Beckett in terms that present it as more animal than human. The children are, for instance, described as a 'litter'. Such caricatural anti-Catholicism is as problematic as the forms of cultural nationalism against which Beckett so often rails. Following on from his identification of Belacqua in *More Pricks Than Kicks* as a 'dirty low-down Low Church Protestant high-brow', the story of the Lynch family in *Watt* betrays a failure on his part to have worked through his own Irish Protestant cultural origins and prejudices.[9]

While the national-cultural signifiers are far less prevalent in *Watt* than in his earlier works, and while the novel constitutes a first significant step towards a new kind of writing that might even be termed post-national, Beckett nonetheless continues here to engage in a form of culture war. The story of the Lynch family is a case in point, as is the passage on the virility drug Bando, the name of which is derived from the French verb *bander*: to have an erection. The reader is informed that Bando has been banned by the state:

---

[9] In this matter, see, in particular, Houston (2018) and Kennedy (2019).

For the State, taking as usual the law into its own hands, and duly indifferent to the sufferings of thousands of men, and tens of thousands of women, all over the country, has seen fit to place an embargo on this admirable article, from which joy could stream, at a moderate cost, into homes, and other places of rendez-vous, now desolate. It cannot enter our ports, nor cross our northern frontier, if not in the form of a casual, hazardous and surreptitious dribble. (146)

That northern border is evidently the border between Éire and Northern Ireland.

The story of Mr Ernest Louit, author of a study entitled *The Mathematical Intuitions of the Visicelts*, differs from the story of the Lynch family 'litter' in that it constitutes a comic attack on racist forms of cultural nationalism (146ff). As C. J. Ackerley observes, in the fictional Visicelts, Beckett is playing on the distinction between two Germanic tribes, the Ostogoths (or Eastern Goths) and the Visigoths (Western Goths) (see Ackerley, 2005, 160). Louit's study clearly falls into the tradition of nationalist race theory that emerged in the second half of the nineteenth century. It is an attempt to demonstrate that the authentically Irish people – the Visicelts, or Western Celts – have superior powers of mathematical intuition. While the story of the Lynch family 'litter' is simply an attack on Irish Catholic culture, the story of Louit's research into the Visicelts takes a step back, mocking, as it does, precisely the kind of race theory that lay at the heart of the Nazi ideology of the supposedly superior racial type: the Aryan, an idea to which Beckett would return in *Malone Dies*.

It is worth bearing in mind that the passages in *Watt* on the Lynch family and the Visicelts were written at a time when the Nazi death camps in Eastern Europe were in full operation. *Watt* was completed in May 1945. Buchenwald, near Weimar, was liberated on 11 April 1945; Bergen Belsen, in Lower Saxony, on 15 April 1945; and Dachau, near Munich, on 26 April 1945. Then, in June 1945, Beckett learned of the death of his friend Alfred Péron, who had assisted him in the translation into French of *Murphy*, and who, as a member of the same Resistance cell as Beckett (Gloria SMH), had been arrested by the Gestapo in August 1942 and imprisoned in Mauthausen concentration camp. What is particularly striking about *Watt* is that it contains a ridiculing of racist-nationalist theory in the story of Louit, as well as a highly problematic mocking of Irish Catholic culture grounded in a vision of Irish Catholics as a proliferating, animalistic mass – in other words, as something troublingly similar to the Nazi conception of the Jews. The novel reveals just how difficult it is to free oneself from the very forms of cultural bias that Beckett was seeking to challenge.

With the liberation of the Nazi concentration camps across Continental Europe, the full horror of that most extreme form of racial cultural nationalism was exposed to the eyes of the world's media. In the years immediately following the end of the war, a series of important works began to reveal the full scale of the horror. One of the first was David Rousset's *L'Univers concentrationnaire* (1945), which won the Prix Renaudot in 1946. Beckett's own view of cultural nationalism had arisen in an Ireland in which there were no concentration camps, but in which there was censorship, to which his unpublished broadside 'Censorship in the Saorstat' had testified. As we have seen, this Ireland-focused anti-cultural nationalism continued to play an important role in Beckett's fiction until the end of the Second World War. In part as a result of his experiences in London (1934–6) and then in Germany (1936–7), Beckett's views on cultural nationalism broadened considerably, as evidenced in particular by his remarks in the letters he wrote to MacGreevy from Germany on the Nazis' anti-Semitic cultural nationalism. And yet, *Watt* includes comic passages such as the story of the Lynch family 'litter' that make for highly distasteful reading, especially when one considers the wider historical context within which they were written – that is, the period when the Nazi death camps were in full operation, and in which ideas of the 'subhuman' and of peoples who were more animal than human were justifying mass murder across Europe. This is the Beckett who could refer to the Irish people as a 'nameless and hideous mass'. At the same time, it is in *Watt* that another Beckett begins to emerge; namely, a writer who would attempt to move beyond the easy but profoundly questionable wins of caricatural representations of particular cultures. This is the Beckett who grasps that the way beyond cultural nationalism lies not in adopting its own stereotyping methods, but rather in embracing a nominalist politics. As we shall see, such a nominalism does not lead to a comfortably cosmopolitan alternative to nationalism.

3 Displaced Persons

Only a few months after the end of the war in Europe, in the 4 August 1945 issue of the *Irish Times*, Beckett published a review of his friend Thomas MacGreevy's recently published book, *Jack B. Yeats: An Appreciation and an Interpretation* (June 1945).[10] Throughout the 1930s, MacGreevy had been Beckett's most intimate correspondent. His letters to MacGreevy provide an invaluable insight into his development during that formative period, and include the March 1934 letter on his own character in which he acknowledged that the 'arrogant "otherness"' that he had cultivated needed to be replaced by

---

[10] Beckett's review was published under the sober title 'MacGreevy on Yeats'.

a form of humility (Beckett, 2009g, 258). As we have seen, Beckett had also championed MacGreevy's early poetry. That said, Beckett was increasingly troubled by what he saw as an ever more pronounced cultural nationalism in MacGreevy's work. As we have seen, on 31 January 1938, shortly after what would prove to be his permanent relocation to France, Beckett informed MacGreevy that, as 'a clot of prejudices', he preferred the first half of the latter's work, 'with its real and radiant individuals, to the second, with our national scene' (Beckett, 2009g, 600). Beckett himself would have to struggle to embrace the nominalist spirit of this comment, the national-cultural stereotypes continuing to appear in his own work – in *Watt*, for instance. As for MacGreevy's book on Yeats, it had been completed in January 1938, its publication then being postponed until the end of the Second World War, with a postscript added in April 1945.

Beckett's critical distance from MacGreevy's cultural nationalism found its first public airing in his review of the latter's book on Yeats. There can be no doubt that by 1938 MacGreevy had adopted a profoundly cultural-nationalist view of art. He had come to believe that 'the artist is the truest register of the spirit of the community to which he belongs' (MacGreevy, 1945, 32). Moreover: 'The artist, poet or painter perceives and in terms of the imagination projects, the idea that the people to whom he belongs have of themselves, and thus creates the attitude that the world will have of them afterwards' (34). In other words, a nation's cultural self-image is to be disseminated through art. As is almost always the case in nationalist appeals to the 'people' or to the 'will of the people', it is soon clear that MacGreevy had a very particular version of that people in mind. Diversity and inclusivity are rarely at the heart of any appeal to the idea of a national culture. While Benedict Anderson is right to insist that nationalism conceives of the nation as limited, in the sense of it not including all of humanity and of being set in the context of other (rival) nations, it is no less true that nationalism also tends to discriminate within the nation-state between those who belong properly to it, even incarnating it, and those who do not. This latter discrimination is certainly present in MacGreevy's book on Yeats. For, according to MacGreevy, Yeats's paintings represented not simply the Irish scene, but 'the Ireland that matters' (5). His was 'the Ireland that has always most mattered and always will most matter, the true and good and beautiful Ireland that, to put it very simply, has a heart' (33). There were thus two Irelands – one that mattered and one that did not, one to be cherished and one to be dismissed.

The Irish who mattered, according to MacGreevy, were those who had been the 'under-dog', the 'conquered people of Ireland', those who had not benefited from any genuine form of 'self-expression' until the advent of 'the modern art of painting' (8). His conception of the Irish was populist in the sense that it was limited to what he termed the *'petit peuple'*, this being the social group whose lives were represented in Yeats's paintings, rather than that of any elite (9). They included the 'strollers, tinkers, gypsies and tramps of every kind', all of whom Yeats treated 'seriously' and with 'respect' (35). These, according to MacGreevy, were the 'Irish Irish', to be distinguished, as he went on to make clear, from the 'Anglo-Irish'. This was a profoundly divisive conception of the Irish people, since it did not include all of those who had been born in Ireland. While acknowledging that Jack B. Yeats himself was 'Anglo-Irish by origin', MacGreevy insisted that the painter belonged to that 'small, generous-minded minority of Anglo-Irishmen' who, influenced by the French Revolution, 'had been friendly to the people ever since the days of Wolfe Tone and Edward Fitzgerald' (20–1).

Yeats was not, MacGreevy argued, simply part of an artistic tradition that had captured the life of the 'Irish Irish'. His uniqueness was absolute, there being 'no trace of even remotely approximate imitation of other painters in his work' (10). While he belonged to a tradition extending back to Wolfe Tone of Anglo-Irishmen who recognized that they themselves did not belong to the 'Irish Irish', while nonetheless fighting for it,[11] he was nonetheless the first 'genuine artist' to have 'so identified himself with the people of Ireland as to be able to give true and good and beautiful artistic expression to the life they lived, and to that sense of themselves as the Irish nation' (10). What, one might reasonably ask, is a 'genuine' artist, and how does that figure differ from the inauthentic? The answer exposes the circular logic of MacGreevy's argument. For it is clear that Yeats was a 'genuine' artist precisely because he depicted the life of the 'Irish Irish' as that of a nation. If he had peers, they were not in Ireland but on the Continent, in the shape of other foundational nation-expressing artists such as Rembrandt, Velázquez, and Watteau. Like them, Yeats was, he asserted, not merely a 'national painter', but *'the* national painter', in that his work was 'the consummate expression of the spirit of his own nation at one of the supreme points in its evolution' (10). MacGreevy proceeded to single out the painting *Going to Wolfe Tone's Grave* (1929) as a work in which 'the national note is struck as clearly as ever in the past' (37).

As is so often the case in nationalist arguments regarding a particular culture, the national proved conveniently here also to be the universal. Notwithstanding (and indeed precisely on account of) its focus on the 'Irish Irish', Yeats's art was, according to MacGreevy, characterized by a 'universality of outlook' (39). Just as MacGreevy took the part for the whole when he asserted that the *'petit*

---

[11] Wolfe Tone (1763–98) was one of the leaders of the Irish Rebellion of 1798.

peuple' were the true people of Ireland, so he generalized to make them representative of the whole of humanity. As he put it of the Irish strollers, tinkers, gypsies, and tramps: 'They were symbolical of the whole human odyssey. The world, after all, is no more than a temporary camping place, to which men come, and from which they go, like travelling tinkers' (35). Indeed, he considered Yeats's art to be concerned, precisely in its representation of the 'Irish Irish', with universal 'human values' (11). Yeats's humanism was evident in his treating his figures within a landscape that was never simply a background, but that did not dominate either. Rather, there was, MacGreevy argued, a 'humanist' balance achieved between figure and ground, human being and landscape. This set Yeats's art apart from that of John Constable (the quintessential English painter, one can assume), who had 'all but eliminated humanity from the natural scene' (12). This 'new balance' between the human beings and the landscape that they inhabited was one in which 'the landscape is as real as the figures', in that it has 'its own character' (13). Nature here becomes the 'normal environment' in which Yeats depicted the 'Irish Irish' as the true representatives of humanity (12). While the landscape was 'impersonal', there was no alienation here between figure and ground. In other words, the landscapes in Yeats's paintings were the true home for his 'Irish Irish' figures. They belonged in that landscape, and it belonged to them. That landscape was the Irish equivalent of the *Boden* so celebrated by the Nazis.

According to MacGreevy, the universality of Yeats's culturally national art was also reflected in its scenes capturing a history that was not strictly speaking its own. As mentioned above, Ireland had opted for neutrality during the Second World War. And yet, MacGreevy asserted, Yeats, as the most national of painters, as an artist concerned above all with the '*petit peuple*', was also representing the horrors of that war. In *Tinkers' Encampment: The Blood of Abel* (1941), for instance, MacGreevy saw Yeats as having depicted 'A world that is dark, a world in which individual human beings are isolated from each other, a world in disorder, above all a world in which blood has been spilt'. And, he asked rhetorically: 'What in 1941 should that mean but the world of war that was all about us?' (36).

Reviewing MacGreevy's book was clearly a challenge for Beckett. As noted above, MacGreevy was undoubtedly among Beckett's most intimate correspondents during the 1930s. He shared more of his inner life in his letters to MacGreevy than in his correspondence with anyone else during the pre-war years. At the same time, Beckett had also established a close relationship with Jack B. Yeats, and was the proud possessor of one of his paintings, *A Morning*, which he had purchased in May 1936. Significantly, in commenting on this painting in a letter to MacGreevy, he highlighted its capturing for him a sense of liberation from any home: 'It is nice to have Morning on one's wall that is always morning, and a setting out without the coming home' (Beckett, 2009g, 334). Moreover, Beckett's views on cultural nationalism of the kind reflected in MacGreevy's book were longstanding and deeply felt. Indeed, in his own writing he had even at times come to represent the inverted image of such cultural nationalism. As we have seen, he had been guilty of brutally caricatural, stereotyping, and dehumanizing representations of those whom MacGreevy valorized as the 'Irish Irish'. The story of the Lynch family in *Watt* is a case in point.

In his review, Beckett was careful to seek to preserve his friendship with MacGreevy while nonetheless keeping his distance from the nationalist argument at the heart of the latter's book. He began by insisting that MacGreevy had produced art criticism of a 'high order' (Beckett, 1983, 96), and although he surely felt that the nationalist argument was a complete misrepresentation of Yeats's art, he gently asserted that the 'national aspects' of Yeats's 'genius' had merely been 'over-stated' by MacGreevy, as well as by other Irish art critics. As we have seen, MacGreevy placed Yeats in the company of Rembrandt, Velázquez, and Watteau in the pantheon of great national painters, or painters of their nations. According to Beckett, Yeats was indeed to be seen alongside the major European painters, although his choice was far more contemporary than MacGreevy's, including, as it did, Karl Ballmer, Georges Braque, Wassily Kandinsky, Paul Klee, Georges Rouault, and Bram van Velde. But, Beckett insisted, this was not on account of any national element in Yeats's work. Rather, his greatness as an artist lay in the fact that he brought 'light, as only the great dare to bring light, to the issueless predicament of existence' (97). Like MacGreevy, Beckett considered Yeats to capture the nature of humanity as a whole, the signal difference being that this humanity was not something that could be mapped onto any particular nation.

As for Rembrandt, whom MacGreevy identified as another great national painter, Beckett had over a decade earlier made it clear that, in his view, the Dutch master's art achieved something quite different. His greatness as an artist lay, as Beckett put it in *Dream of Fair to Middling Women*, in his achieving in his later self-portraits 'a disfaction, a désuni, an Ungebund, a flottement, a tremblement, a tremor, a tremolo, a disaggregating, a disintegrating, an efflorescence, a breaking down and multiplication of tissue' (Beckett, 1992, 138). In other words, far from affirming any national identity, Rembrandt's art enacted the undoing of all forms of identity and identification. In his late self-portraits, Rembrandt decomposed the very identity of that self, exposing the void on which all sense of identity (including national identity) was constructed.

Beckett's objection to MacGreevy's interpretation of Yeats as a great national painter was lodged in print only months after the end of the war in Europe. A decade later, in his homage to Yeats published in *Les Lettres Nouvelles* in 1954, Beckett reiterated his anti-nationalist take on the painter's work, extending it to all artists of genuine worth: 'The artist who stakes his being', he wrote, 'is from nowhere, has no kith' (Beckett, 1983, 149). In other words, he neither belongs to nor represents a people. This statement reveals the clear direction of travel in Beckett's post-war work, in which, as we shall see, while he rejected all forms of cultural nationalism, he did not embrace the Enlightenment cosmopolitanism of a Boswell or a Voltaire. This break with both nationalism and cosmopolitanism, which was also a break with both Romanticism and the Enlightenment, would be enacted first through a disorientation of all national-cultural identifiers in his principal works of the immediate post-war years.

If the end of the war in Europe was a major historical event for the European nations, it was also a decisive moment in Beckett's own writing life. For it was at that time that he finally turned to French as his principal language of composition. Not only would this decision be the making of him as a writer, but it also bore significantly upon his engagement with ideas of cultural nationalism. In order to appreciate that engagement, it is necessary to ask the following question: What of the culture into which Beckett transplanted himself? To what extent is French culture present in the works written in French? And, more precisely, to what extent might Beckett's post-war work be seen as affirming a form of French cultural nationalism?

It has often been noted that the stichomythia in one of Beckett's first works in French, the short novel *Mercier and Camier* (written between July and October 1946), anticipates the dialogues in *Waiting for Godot*, as does the focus on what, in *The Unnamable*, would later be termed the 'pseudocouple' (Beckett, 2010f, 7). Beckett's works in English had focused on a single figure – Belacqua, Murphy, Watt – whereas in *Mercier and Camier* that figure is disaggregated into a double act. In *Godot* and *Endgame*, the dualities are particularly striking: active/passive, mind/body, master/slave, etc. The style of *Mercier and Camier* also constitutes a significant step towards that writing 'without style' that the Belacqua of *Dream* saw as necessary.

Notwithstanding these similarities between *Mercier and Camier* and Beckett's other works of the later 1940s, there are also some notable differences, which bear directly upon his approach towards the question of cultural nationalism. The names of this pseudocouple can be read as unproblematically French. And while the setting appears to be more Irish than French, it, too, does not involve any of the instabilities consequent upon cross-border movement. While Mercier and Camier embark on a journey, accompanied by their narrator, it is one that entails no crossing of borders, no movement between cultural realms. In short, the two figures remain in their homeland. As the narrator puts it: 'Mercier and Camier did not remove from home, they had that great good fortune. They did not have to face, with greater or lesser success, outlandish ways, tongues, laws, skies, foods, in surroundings little resembling those to which first childhood, then boyhood, then manhood had inured them' (Beckett, 2010c, 3) This is a striking statement in a work written at a time when, across Europe, there had recently been mass displacements of people, forced marches, refugees in unprecedented numbers, and millions of deaths in concentration camps often located far from the victims' homelands. Unlike those many refugees and homeless people, Mercier and Camier not only remain in their homeland, but their journey concludes with a return to their point of departure. Beckett thus gestures here towards that contemporary world of refugees and homelessness through its negation.

The novel also includes references to identifiable European locations. Mercier and Camier recall trips to Rome and Naples, for instance (6). And when, in the final chapter, the figure of Watt reappears, he observes that while he will one day be known (presumably through the publication of the novel Beckett had recently completed), his reputation would not extend to either Ireland or France: 'my notoriety', Watt declares, 'is not likely to penetrate to the denizens of Dublin's fair city, or of Cuq-Toulza', the latter being a town in the Tarn department in the South of France (91). Notwithstanding these and other topographical identifications, the novel does continue the movement towards a less culturally and nationally identifiable realm initiated in *Watt*. Mr Madden, the man whom Mercier and Camier encounter on the train, for instance, states: 'I was born in P—. My parents came from Q—' (29). And Irish as the landscape appears to be – not least on account of its bog – there is a level of abstraction that weakens the identifications.

This weakening is ever more pronounced in the four short stories that Beckett wrote in French between February 1946 and January 1947.[12] The recurring motif in all of these stories is expulsion from a home or a place of refuge or shelter. They are, in short, tales of exposure and unhousing, in this respect clearly echoing recent historical events in Continental Europe. Furthermore, the home from which these figures are expelled is itself far from being a true home. The narrator of 'The Expelled' states, for instance: 'I did not know the town well, scene of my birth and of my first steps' (Beckett, 2009d, 6). The references

---

[12] Of these four stories, the first, 'The End', marks a particularly important step in Beckett's writing life, since it was the first of his post-war prose works to be written in French, although he began it in English, on 17 February 1946, before continuing it in French on 13 March 1946. The transition from English to French thus occurred mid-text, rather than between one work and another.

reflect Beckett's own Continental travels, particularly in Germany – this being a politically significant choice in the immediate post-war years. In 'The Expelled', the narrator recalls visiting the Lüneberg Heath in Lower Saxony (6). The narrator of 'First Love' remembers a visit to Ohlsdorf Cemetery near Hamburg (62), comparing it favourably with the cemetery where his father is buried. In 'The Calmative', there is also an allusion to the medieval German poet Walther von der Vögelweide, when the narrator recalls that, 'Seeing a stone seat by the kerb, I sat down and crossed my legs, like Walther' (29).

Beyond the German, these Continental, ostensibly cosmopolitan references include French history. The narrator of 'The End', for instance, resorts to an expletive already used by Watt: 'Exelmans!' (Beckett, 2009d, 39; 2009j, 181). This is a reference to the Marshal of France René Joseph Isidore Exelmans (1775–1852), who distinguished himself during the retreat of Napoleon's Grande Armée from Moscow in 1812. Why should Beckett introduce this allusion into texts written in the mid-1940s? Albeit subtly, Beckett was locating his work within the context of a brutal modern European history in which nationalism had played such a catastrophic role, from Napoleon's conquest of Continental Europe to Hitler's over a century later. In both cases, the invasion of Russia proved to be catastrophic. The exclamation 'Exelmans!' subtly inscribes that violent history of competing nation-states into Beckett's texts.

If his first sustained efforts in French between February 1946 and January 1947 marked a decisive step away from any clearly identifiable national-cultural frame of reference, it was in the writing of *Molloy* (May–November 1947) that Beckett undertook nothing less than a disorientation of all national-cultural identifications, to the point where it is not even clear how the name of the narrator in Part II of the novel, Moran (first name Jacques), is to be pronounced. In their fine analysis of what they term the 'shifting cultural affinities' in the novel, in its original French, and then in both the English and the German translations, Dirk Van Hulle and Pim Verhulst demonstrate how this disorientation was achieved. Their analysis builds on those by other commentators, including Hill (1990), Morin (2009), and Mooney (2011), who observe that, from a national-cultural perspective, the novel appears to have a 'hybrid status' (Hill, 1990, 40) or 'in-betweenness' (Mooney, 2011, 123). Van Hulle and Verhulst proceed to demonstrate how this was achieved in the textual genesis and the translation of the novel.

There is, however, a considerable difference between something being hybrid – that is, having more than one origin – and its being without any clear origins or context. By describing the sequence of the three novels *Molloy*, *Malone Dies*, and *The Unnamable* both as 'hybrid' and as communicating an 'unmistakable sense of unbelonging', Hill tends to elide this crucial distinction

(1990, 40). The question thus becomes whether *Molloy*, and, indeed, Beckett's bilingual oeuvre as a whole, has two national-cultural homes or none. Does it belong both to an Irish and to a French national culture, to one or the other, or to neither? It is in seeking to address this crucial question that Van Hulle and Verhulst's analysis is particularly helpful. They persuasively characterize the effect achieved by Beckett as one of 'cultural displacement' (Van Hulle and Verhulst, 2020, 31). As we shall see, it is to just such an idea of displacement that Beckett himself will refer over a decade later, when translating the work of the Swiss-born writer Robert Pinget (1919–97).

There are numerous examples of national-cultural disorientation and effacement in *Molloy*. In Part I, Molloy can recall only the first letter of the name of the town from which he originates. In the manuscript, that letter is originally 'D', suggesting Dublin (Van Hulle and Verhulst, 2020, 31; see BDMP4, FN2, 07r).[13] This is subsequently revised to 'B' or 'P', increasing the uncertainty and weakening any national-cultural reference.[14] In the French manuscript, the town of Hole is first named Carrick or Carrig, again suggesting an Irish context (BDMP4, FN3, 90r, 94r; see O'Reilly, Van Hulle, and Verhulst, 2017, 279). And just as these Irish identifiers were removed as the text was revised, so were some of the French. In the French manuscript, the phrase 'ce que les Français appellent une commune' ('what the French call a commune') was ultimately replaced by 'Dans les pays évolués on appelle ça une commune' (Beckett, 1971, 222; see O'Reilly, Van Hulle, and Verhulst, 2017, 261).[15] Similarly, in the expression 'ma putain de patrie' ('my fucking country'), the word 'patrie' (suggesting fatherland) is revised to 'ma région' ('my region'), effacing the language of the national (see BDMP4, FN1, 36r).[16] As it happens, the word 'fatherland' does appear in the published English version, but in a negative construction. Evoking 'the image of old Geulincx' – the Cartesian philosopher whose *Ethics* Beckett had read with such interest when writing *Murphy* a decade earlier – and the figure of Ulysses, Molloy reflects: 'And from the poop, poring upon the wave, a sadly rejoicing slave, I follow with my eyes the proud and futile wake. Which, as it bears me from no fatherland [*nulle patrie*] away, bears me onward to no shipwreck' (Beckett, 2009h, 50; 1971, 82).

---

[13] References to the BDMP are to the online modules of the Beckett Digital Manuscript Project. See www.beckettarchive.org.

[14] The published English version reads: 'I felt sure that it began with a B or a P, but in spite of this clue, or perhaps because of its falsity, the other letters continued to escape me' (Beckett, 2009h, 29).

[15] The published English version reads: 'In modern countries this is what I think is called a commune' (Beckett, 2009h, 139). The French might equally have been translated as 'developed countries', and it is striking that Beckett chose 'modern' over 'developed'.

[16] The published English version reads: 'my part of the world', which is even less concrete (Beckett, 2009h, 50).

Considering these and other examples, Van Hulle and Verhulst conclude that Beckett sought to achieve a 'cultural destabilization', both in the writing of the original French version of *Molloy* and in the English translation. This destabilization does not result in a binary or bipolar text, pointing to two national-cultural contexts simultaneously. While there are elements that do seem to result in such a binary national-cultural identification, there are also elements that point, in Beckett's words, to 'no fatherland', and to a genuine experience of non-belonging. For instance, while the proper names Molloy and Jacques Moran appear to point towards two identifiable national-cultural worlds, one Irish and the other French, names such as Lousse are considerably more disorientating (see O'Reilly, Van Hulle, and Verhulst, 2017, 189).

That said, Beckett could not resist resorting on occasion to his former mockery of what MacGreevy termed the 'Irish Irish' and Beckett the 'nameless and hideous mass'. For instance, in 'The End' the narrator declares that 'It was all Greek to me' in response to the political discourse of a man in the street 'haranguing the passers-by' on the political themes of 'Union ... brothers ... Marx ... capital ... bread and butter ... love' (Beckett, 2009d, 52). The phrase 'It was all Greek to me' translates the neutral French 'Je n'y comprenais rien' ('I didn't understand any of it') (Beckett, 1987, 102). In *Molloy*, however, on the subject of the difference between tears and laughter, Molloy declares: 'they are so much Gaelic to me' (2009h, 35). This swipe at the Irish language was added in translation, the original French reading simply: 'je ne m'y connais guère' (Beckett, 1971, 58). The idea of Gaelic as that which is the most foreign is clearly one that remained with Beckett, for, in a letter to Hans Naumann some years later (17 February 1954), he stated: 'I do not consider English a foreign language, it is my language. If there is one that is really foreign to me, it is Gaelic' (Beckett, 2011, 464).

That Gaelic should be seen in this way testifies to Beckett's ongoing failure to keep his distance from the culturally nationalist environment in which he had grown up. He could not resist targeted attacks on that particular world, even as he sought to extricate his work from it by moving towards a more abstract representation. There can, however, be no doubt that he was struggling to achieve precisely that. One further example of this tendency in *Molloy* is Beckett's decision to excise the long passage in Part II on the economy of Ballyba, centred as that economy was around excrement (see O'Reilly, Van Hulle, and Verhulst, 2017, 262ff). Adam Winstanley has argued convincingly that this passage was a satire on the Irish Taoiseach Éamon de Valera's advocacy of a protectionist self-sufficient economy (see Winstanley, 2014, 97). As it happens, this recalls Fichte's early-nineteenth-century nationalist idea of the closed commercial state. According to Fichte:

> It is clear that in a nation that has been closed off in this way, with members living only among themselves and as little as possible with strangers, obtaining their particular way of life, institutions, and morals from these measures and faithfully loving their fatherland and everything patriotic, there will soon arise a high degree of national honor and a sharply determined national character. (Fichte, 2012, 195)

Beckett's ridiculing of such an economy in the manuscript of *Molloy* is of a piece with his attitude to cultural nationalism more generally. His decision not to include it in the published version of the novel does not contradict that attitude; rather, it reveals Beckett struggling to occupy a new space, one located beyond the competing positions of protectionism and the free market, nationalism and internationalism.

References to French national culture increase in the two novels that Beckett wrote after *Molloy*. Indeed, in retrospect, the two parts of *Molloy* appear to mark the transition from a more Irish- to a more French-facing approach, with the name Jacques Moran signalling this shift. *Malone Dies* (written between November 1947 and May 1948) opens with a reference to 'the Fourteenth of July, festival of freedom' (Beckett, 2010b, 3), this being, of course, the French National Day, commemorating the storming of the Bastille and the beginning of the French Revolution. However, in the context of Beckett's novel, it is associated not with any form of political freedom, but rather with the freedom that Malone sees as lying in his own death: 'I shall soon be quite dead at last, in spite of all' (3). Political liberation is replaced here by existential liberation, the added irony lying in the fact that the liberation of the (very few) prisoners in the Bastille was soon followed by an upsurge in nationalist sentiment in France that would in due course lead to the coming to power of Napoleon, whose eventual demise had already been subtly alluded to by Beckett through the exclamation 'Exelmans!' in *Watt* and 'The End'.

In *The Unnamable* (written between March 1949 and January 1950), the narrator mentions the famous Prix Goncourt in the French original, this being revised to the Pulitzer Prize in the English translation (Beckett, 2010f, 96), there being at the time no equally prestigious literary prize in England or Ireland. For all the strangeness of the setting, the narrator does locate himself at one point in an identifiably French locale: stuck in a vase outside a restaurant on the Rue Brancion in Paris's fifteenth arrondissement, where he was watered by a woman named sometimes Madeleine and sometimes Marguerite (57). Why the Rue Brancion, of all possible Parisian locations? There are doubtless various reasons to be considered, one of which points again to French military history: the street in question was named (in 1864) after the French colonel Adolphe-Ernest Raguet de Brancion, who was killed in action at the Battle of Malakoff in

1855, during the Crimean War, when the French army attacked the Russian forces on the Malakoff redoubt at Sevastopol.

In the three post-war novels, the reader encounters a disorientating range of national-cultural references, with inversions of traditional meanings (for instance, Bastille Day being associated with the freedom of death) and an increasing sense less of Irish/French hybridity or bipolarity than of national-cultural non-belonging. At the same time, the violence associated with nationalism is subtly inscribed into these three novels, and this continues to be the case in the works written in the subsequent decade, most notably, as we shall see, in the play *Endgame*.

As for Beckett's decision to explore playwriting, his first attempt in French could not have been more different from his one sustained attempt in English prior to the outbreak of the war. Having completed *Murphy*, and before embarking on the writing of *Watt*, he had taken substantial notes for, and even commenced writing, a play entitled *Human Wishes*, in which the historical specificity could not be clearer: Samuel Johnson's trials and tribulations resulting from his love for the writer Hester Lynch Salusbury (1741–1821). In his first attempt at a play in French, *Eleutheria* (written in January and February 1947) – the title being the Greek word for 'freedom' – Beckett did not break with such cultural-historical specificity, setting the play in contemporary Paris, with references to Passy and the Impasse de l'Enfant-Jésus, for instance (Beckett, 1996, 18–19). That said, he took full advantage of the opportunities for cross-linguistic puns that explode any coherent sense of a national-cultural context. The characters have names such as Krap, Piouk, and Skunk, all of which have no particular meaning in French but do in English, evoking excrement, vomit, and stench. More importantly, the play marks a step beyond the attacks on Irish Catholic culture to be found in Beckett's English-language works.

At the heart of *Eleutheria* are two negative conceptions of the human, one represented by the sinister Dr André Piouk, who, his wife declares, is 'especially interested in humanity' (14), and the other by the play's protagonist, Victor Krap. Although a doctor, Dr Piouk proves to have more in common with the Nazi doctors who had recently carried out appalling experiments in the concentration camps than with those who abide by the Hippocratic oath. Dr Piouk's 'solution' to what he terms the 'problem of humanity' proves to be sterilization and euthanasia (44–5). One needs to bear in mind the historical context in which these ideas were being expressed – precisely two years after the liberation of Auschwitz. And, as if to bring home the connection, Beckett even includes references to barbed wire in the play, with M. Krap saying of his home: 'The flat will soon be covered in barbed wire' (40–1). Dr Piouk is keen to help the depressed Victor to die. After all, he declares, 'We are no longer living in the Third Republic' (113). What becomes clear, however, is that he has completely failed to grasp what it is that Victor desires, namely a freedom both from others and from the self that is neither the freedom of death nor the freedom that the Nazis had so recently, and so cynically, offered to those it imprisoned in its concentration camps; namely, freedom through work, 'Arbeit macht frei' being the inscription in iron above the gates to Auschwitz. The freedom of which Victor Krap dreams is rather the freedom to do and to be nothing. It is the pursuit of this absolute freedom that leads him at the end of the play to turn his 'emaciated back' not simply on Ireland, but on 'humanity' (170). Thus, while both Dr Piouk and Victor Krap hate the human, the former wishes to annihilate others and the latter to negate the self.

Seen in its historical context, *Eleutheria* is a profoundly disturbing work. It was written at a time when the full horror of the Nazi reign of terror had recently been exposed, with many millions having been murdered either in the death camps or by Einsatzgruppen on the Eastern Front. And yet, in that very context, Beckett was prepared to write a play in which he not only mocked the inhumanity represented by Dr Piouk and suggested a connection between the existentially tormented Victor and those 'emaciated' victims in the Nazi concentration camps, but also explored the idea of turning one's back on humanity. While rejecting the forms of nationalism that had culminated in such brutality, he was not prepared to embrace an internationalist or cosmopolitan humanism. In this, he took his distance from Jean-Paul Sartre, among others. His conception of human freedom could not have been more different from that being expressed by Sartre at the very same time, in *Existentialism and Humanism* (1946).[17]

Whereas in *Eleutheria* the proper names serve a translinguistic purpose, denigrating the characters through associating them with excrement and vomit, in Beckett's next play, *Waiting for Godot* (written between October 1948 and January 1949), they achieve an altogether different effect. While some of the proper names in the play suggest a French setting, they do not signify any kind of identification with French national culture. As for the names of the dramatis personae, they suggest a world of refugees, migrants, or displaced persons. There is the Russian-named Vladimir, the Italian-named Pozzo, the English/Irish/ American- (and decidedly ironically) named Lucky, the French-named Estragon (the French word for the herb tarragon), and the unnamed, generically identified Boy. In the original French manuscript, Vladimir's companion is called not Estragon, but Lévy, a Jewish name that, according to Angela Moorjani, in Hebrew means 'attached to' (see Moorjani, 2009, 7). The name is thus at once entirely appropriate, since Lévy is attached to Vladimir in one more

---

[17] On the theme of Beckett and humanism, see, for instance, Weller (2020).

'pseudocouple', and also entirely inappropriate, or ironic, since he is without any national-cultural attachments. Moreover, as Van Hulle and Verhulst observe, when the Russian-named Vladimir tells the Jewish-named Lévy that, but for him, the latter would be 'nothing more than a little heap of bones at the present minute' (cf. Beckett, 2010g, 6), this would (in the late 1940s) inevitably have brought to mind the liberation of the Nazi death camps in Eastern Europe by the Soviet army only a few years earlier (see Van Hulle and Verhulst, 2017a, 173). As noted above, Auschwitz was liberated by the Russians in January 1945, less than three years before Beckett began work on the play.

In the play's dialogue, there are a number of passing references to French place-names, including Roussillon, in the Vaucluse, where Beckett had taken refuge during the Nazi occupation of northern France, and, in Lucky's dialogue, to Seine-et-Marne and Normandy, where in 1945 Beckett had worked at the Irish Red Cross Hospital in Saint-Lô. Mention is also made of the Eiffel Tower, from which the hapless Vladimir and Estragon might, the former reflects, have done better to throw themselves many years before. Nothing could be more clearly a marker of France, and indeed of French national culture, than the Eiffel Tower. There was nothing coincidental about these references. As Beckett wrote in a letter to his American publisher Barney Rosset regarding his English translation of the play: 'I tried to retain the French atmosphere as much as possible and you may have noticed that the use of English and American place-names is confined to Lucky whose own name might seem to justify them' (Beckett, 2011, 398). So it was that Seine-et-Marne and Normandy became Fulham Clapham and Connemara, respectively, in the English translation (Beckett, 2010g, 41), while the Durance became the Rhône (51), presumably because it would be more familiar to an English-language audience. Thus, whereas the French version tends to limit its references to France, the English-language text points both to Ireland and to England, as well as to France.

The Eiffel Tower, that most familiar of all symbols of French national culture, is associated in *Godot* not with French cultural grandeur, however, but rather with a missed opportunity to commit suicide. The association with death of this cultural signifier of French national culture par excellence clearly echoes the association of the Fourteenth of July (Bastille Day) with Malone's death in *Malone Dies*. The Durance, in south-east France, is also mentioned in relation to suicide: Vladimir recalls having thrown himself into the river, and not for a swim or a bath. While retaining a number of national-cultural signifiers, *Godot* tends to disorient them in a manner akin to *Molloy*, while also much more clearly evoking a world of the homeless. Rather than being cosmopolitans, Vladimir and Estragon are displaced persons, migrants, refugees.

In his next major play, *Endgame* (the genesis of which was both challenging and protracted, and which he completed in September 1956), Beckett took a decisive step away even from the disorientating national references to be found in *Molloy* and *Godot*, to a world as stripped of such affiliations as that of *The Unnamable*. This lag in his dramatic works reflected Beckett's tendency to be more conservative aesthetically when first engaging with a new genre or medium.[18] *Endgame*'s 'bare interior' is detached from any clear historical or topographical context, these having been largely removed during the work's genesis.[19] That said, the published versions in both French and English do retain references to suffering, violence, and death by way of allusions to political nationalism. Indeed, they are more pointed than in Beckett's earlier works in French.

The characters Nagg and Nell, now confined to dustbins, recall losing their legs in a bicycle accident that occurred on the way to Sedan in north-east France. The passage in question reads:

NAGG: Do you remember—
NELL: No.
NAGG: When we crashed our tandem and lost our shanks. [*They laugh heartily.*]
NELL: It was in the Ardennes. [*They laugh less heartily.*]
NAGG: On the road to Sedan. [*They laugh still less heartily.*][20]

On the one hand, this reference to Sedan and the Ardennes in north-eastern France, on the border with Belgium and Germany, might be read as random: any other place-names would have done as well. On the other hand, however, they can be seen to allude to major historical events that would shape the entire twentieth century and beyond, events arising out of nineteenth-century European nationalism. In the Franco-Prussian War of 1870–1, the French Emperor Napoleon III's forces suffered a devastating defeat at Sedan, and this Prussian victory over the French would soon be followed by the siege of Paris and the unification of the German states into a new Reich. Seventy years later, in what became known as the Second Battle of Sedan in May 1940, Hitler's forces overran the French army at Sedan, paving the way for the defeat of France in the Second World War and Beckett's own desperate flight south from the Nazi

---

[18] Other examples of this include Beckett's first radio play, *All That Fall* (written in August and September 1956, while he was trying to complete *Endgame*), in which he adopted a clearly identifiable Irish setting and a realist manner; and his first play for television, *Eh Joe* (written in April and May 1965).

[19] On the genesis of *Endgame*, see Van Hulle and Weller (2018).

[20] Beckett (2009c, 13). For a more detailed analysis of this passage, see Van Hulle and Weller (2018, 321–2).

occupiers. As for the Ardennes, between December 1944 and January 1945 it would be the site of the last major German offensive of the Second World War. The failure of this offensive effectively marked the end of any serious German resistance to the Allied forces in Western Europe, and was soon followed by the total collapse of Nazi Germany.

Rather than being merely incidental references to a French context, it is modern Europe's dark history that is subtly inscribed into one of Beckett's darkest plays through these references to Sedan and the Ardennes as the place where two of the characters suffered life-changing mutilations. From the Franco-Prussian War to the Second World War, what is captured in Beckett's choice of place-names here is the catastrophic consequences of the forms of Romantic nationalism that emerged in the early nineteenth century, finding their first articulation in works such as Fichte's *Addresses to the German Nation*. It is also striking that Beckett includes a reference to the (Russian) steppe in *Endgame*, again evoking a place of suffering in modern European history, shaped as that history was by precisely the forms of nationalism that Beckett was seeking to reject, without ever taking refuge in a comfortable cosmopolitanism.

A particularly revealing document with regard to Beckett's engagement with the question of cultural nationalism and its alternatives at this point in his writing life is his translation (or, as it is identified in the published version, adaptation) of Robert Pinget's play *La Manivelle* (1960). In September 1959, Pinget was asked by Barbara Bray, who at the time was working for the BBC, to write a radio play specifically for the Corporation. Pinget decided to turn a scene from his current work-in-progress – the novel *Clope au dossier* (1961) – into a dialogue for radio. The scene in question features two old men reminiscing about a past that they have considerable difficulty recollecting with any degree of accuracy, and reflecting on the changing times and the fate of the people they once knew. As soon as he had drafted the dialogue, Pinget showed it to Beckett, whose enthusiastic reaction Pinget recorded in a typescript entitled 'Notre ami Samuel Beckett', which he had been inspired to write as the equivalent of James Boswell's *Life of Johnson* (1791).[21] As Pinget went on to record, Beckett 'transposed the French atmosphere into an Anglo-Irish atmosphere. My two very French wrecks became two Irishmen installed in London. Sam asked my permission to make this transposition and even to change the names' ('Notre ami', 22).

---

[21] As Pinget put it: 'He liked it so much that he immediately offered to translate it into English' ('Notre ami', 21–2). For a more extended analysis of Beckett's 'adaptation' (rather than translation) of *La Manivelle*, see Weller (2015).

A draft translation completed, Beckett wrote to Pinget on 30 November 1959 to inform him that Barbara Bray had read and very much enjoyed the translation (entitled *The Old Tune*), but that she had noted 'certain anomalies'. The precise nature of those anomalies was communicated in a letter to Pinget dated 13 December 1959, in which Beckett wrote: 'They are asking me: where are these men? In Ireland? In England? If in England, whence this language? If in Ireland, why these place names? Etc. That's the piddling sort of thing. They are in England and they talk like that' (Beckett, 2014, 265). No doubt Beckett, who had lived in London in the mid-1930s, and had mentioned this to Pinget in an earlier letter, was more than a little put out by the confusion created by his having placed an Irishman in London. It is telling that this should have been seen as an 'anomaly' by those at the home of British broadcasting.

On 6 February 1960, Beckett sent Pinget what he described as his 'impertinent translation final state'. On 16 February 1960, he reported that Bray was 'very happy with the revised "translation"' of *La Manivelle* (Beckett, 2014, 302). Beckett's placing of the word 'translation' in inverted commas clearly signalled his growing sense of its problematic status. When it was published together with Pinget's original text by their shared French publisher, Les Éditions de Minuit, the cover and title page avoided 'translated by', in favour of 'English text by Samuel Beckett' (*texte anglais de Samuel Beckett*). When the Calder edition of *The Old Tune* appeared in 1963, it was identified as an 'Adaptation by Samuel Beckett'.

If one compares *The Old Tune* with *La Manivelle*, it is immediately evident that the English text is in many respects a translation – and a very fine one – of the French. Indeed, it is for the most part just as respectful of the original French as are Beckett's English translations of his own work. That said, while it does not cut anything from the text (as Beckett's self-translations sometimes do), it departs from the norms of translation in a number of key respects. Of these, the most immediately striking is – to allude to the 'Addendum' of *Watt* – the fact that Beckett decided to 'change all the names' (Beckett, 2009j, 222). Proper names are generally immune in translation. One would not expect, for instance, to read a translation of Kafka's *Die Verwandlung* in which Gregor Samsa is rendered as Gregory Samsa.[22] In his rendering of *La Manivelle* into English, however, Beckett broke with this immunity of the proper name to translation. In the original French, in addition to the names of the two main characters, Toupin and Pommard (rendered as Gorman and Cream in the English), there are thirty-three other named persons, all of whose names are either anglicized or replaced

---

[22] That said, in J. A. Underwood's translation of *Die Verwandlung* (*The Metamorphosis*) Gregor is indeed rendered as Gregory (see Kafka, 1995, 91–146).

by an English name in Beckett's version. In addition, there are also eight place-names, all of which are changed to suggest an English setting. The play also contains the names of various businesses and other establishments, all of which are anglicized, as is the name of a newspaper mentioned in passing.[23] In this process of radical anglicization, only a few of the name changes reveal Beckett attempting to capture any semantic potential in the original. The exceptions include Bacon for Descartes, Wellington for Talleyrand, and Plumpton for Boulette. Clearly, what Beckett was seeking to achieve through all these name changes was a version that would strike the English auditor or reader as familiar in its setting and range of reference. In other words, there is nothing in the English version to suggest that the work comes from a French context. Crucially, however, the range of English names and the English setting are at odds with the Irishisms and Irish accent of one of the characters in the original BBC broadcast.

By having one of the two speakers (Gorman) adopt an Irish idiom and accent in an English setting, Beckett was alluding to his own experience as an (alienated) Irishman in London almost three decades earlier, while finding an equivalent for the Savoyard nature of the character in Pinget's play. In so doing, he was being faithful not only to Pinget's play but also to Pinget's own personal experience in France, that is, as a speaker of the 'national' language whose Swiss-French speech marked him out as neither completely foreign nor completely native. As Beckett put it in a letter to Barbara Bray on 1 December 1959, he had been struck by what he termed the 'displaced persons quality' of Pinget's characters. He considered this quality to have been captured in the French text, and had sought to find its equivalent in English through a reliance upon 'Irish rhythms and inversions'. The Irishisms in Beckett's English adaptation of *La Manivelle* include adjectives such as 'grand', 'darling', and 'gallous' (Beckett, 2009a, 155, 156, 163), and phrases such as 'more power to you' (155). As Beckett noted in his letter to Bray on 1 December, the English text was also marked by recurrent syntactical inversions where there are none in the French, examples including 'gallous garage they have there near the slaughterhouse' (163). The historical irony here is that the 'displaced persons' in this play recall their time in the British Army, 'in the Foot, at Chatham', and Gorman even has 'happy memories' of their mobilization at the time of the First World War (Beckett, 2009a, 160).

Beckett was thus seeking to achieve a version of Pinget's play in English that would capture that 'displaced persons quality' he had detected in the language

---

[23] For the full list, see Weller (2015, 39 n. 37, 38, 39). For Beckett's attempts to find English alternatives, see his 'Été 56' notebook, UoR MS 1227–7–7–1, Beckett International Foundation, University of Reading.

of the original. That quality marked a departure from the norms of the 'national' language, be it French or English. And, of course, the point being made was that French is also the language of those, such as Pinget, who are not French citizens, just as Beckett's English was not that of a British citizen. Those so-called national languages are in fact as heterogeneous, as much of a mixture, as Defoe's 'true-born Englishman' or Beckett's 'trueborn Jackeen'. What is generally seen as a minor work in the Beckett canon proves to play an important role in his ongoing resistance to forms of cultural nationalism, not least those that are manifest in the idea of a national language. Both thematically and stylistically, his post-war works explore the experience of displaced persons for whom there is no homeland and no language with which they can fully identify, such identifications being exposed as forms of violence.

4 Citizens of Nowhere

In a speech delivered in October 2016, shortly after the referendum on the United Kingdom's membership of the European Union, the then British prime minister, Theresa May, declared: 'If you believe you are a citizen of the world you are a citizen of nowhere.' According to May, in what was a radical rejection of one of the core ideas of the European Enlightenment, there is no such thing as genuine cosmopolitanism. The notion of being a citizen of nowhere, of lacking any binding affiliation to a particular nation-state, was clearly meant to be understood by the British public as among the worst of all possible fates. Ironically, the British prime minister could not have found a better phrase to describe Beckett's conception of the artist or, indeed, many of the figures in his later works of prose fiction and drama. As we have seen, in his 1954 homage to the work of Jack B. Yeats, he had insisted that 'The artist who stakes his being is from nowhere, has no kith.' As for the figures in Beckett's later prose fiction (from *How It Is* onwards), they are often stripped of all, or almost all, national-cultural affiliations. What sometimes survives this radically ascetic approach to the cultural is Christian imagery and symbolism, which, while certainly present in the early works, becomes more evident in some of Beckett's later works precisely because so much else has been removed. This is not, however, to suggest that Beckett's is a Christian or even a religious art. Rather, it is to highlight the fact that Beckett's approach to cultural nationalism does not extend to a consistent abstraction away from the Christian culture of the West.[24]

As we have seen, the stripping away of the signs of national-cultural belonging was far from complete even in *The Unnamable*. With *How It Is* (written between December 1958 and August 1960), however, Beckett opted for

---

[24] On Beckett and Christianity, see, in particular, Tonning (2014, ch. 4).

a setting that was not to be found on any political map of the world, but rather a place akin to one of the circles in Dante's *Inferno*. The world where national-cultural signifiers would have any meaning becomes that 'other' life, lived 'above in the light', and belonging very much to the past. The climactic event in *How It Is* is the encounter with Pim, a name akin to Bim and Bom, to whom Beckett had already referred in the story 'Yellow', in *More Pricks Than Kicks*, and then in manuscript drafts of *Waiting for Godot* and *Endgame*, before they resurfaced in *How It Is* and then in one of Beckett's last works, the television play *What Where*. Beckett explained that Bim and Bom had been comedians in Stalinist Russia. However, these names, as well as others such as Prim, Krim, Kram, Skom, and Skum in *How It Is*, are clearly chosen in part because they bear no clear national-cultural affiliation. They are, in short, the names of citizens of nowhere. While the concrete references that are to be found in *How It Is* point to a Christian culture, they do not point to a particular national culture. Mention is made, for instance, of the Apostles' Creed, Lent, and Hallowmas (Beckett, 2009e, 11–12), but, in Part 2 of the novel, even the recollection of scraps of Pim's life above in the light is lacking in national-cultural detail. He remembers that he did 'a little of everything', that his father was possibly in the 'building trade', and that his mother was a 'column of jade bible invisible in the black hand' (67). While there is arguably an autobiograph-ical dimension here, it does not serve to locate the scene within a particular national culture.

That is not to suggest, however, that *How It Is* does not engage with the political. The very violence of the text, in which the impact of Beckett's attentive and enthusiastic reading of the Marquis de Sade in the 1930s is evident, speaks to the political history of Beckett's time.[25] The recollections of a past life are filled with violence. The narrator recalls, for instance, having 'scissored into slender strips the wings of butterflies first one wing then the other sometimes for a change the two abreast never so good since' (Beckett, 2009e, 5). And then there is the violence, both verbal and physical, directed at Pim as he is tortured into speech in the name of love. And most disturbingly of all, that violence is often associated with pleasure. While Beckett avoids any explicit association between this violence and the violence of twentieth-century history, including the two world wars through which he had lived, it is nonetheless the case that he wrote the novel at the height of the Algerian War of Independence, during which torture was employed by both sides.[26] There is ample evidence that Beckett was deeply troubled by that conflict, its

---

[25] On Beckett's sustained engagement with Sade, see Rabaté (2020).
[26] On the impact of the Algerian War on Beckett, see Morin (2017, ch. 4).

impact being felt close to home when his publisher, Jerôme Lindon, became a terrorist target for publishing a volume critical of the French military's reliance on torture in Algeria. In *How It Is*, Beckett refers in passing to 'empires that are born and die as though nothing had happened' (8). At the moment he wrote those words, France itself was in the process of losing what remained of its colonial empire, following its defeat in Indo-China and the worsening situation in Algeria. There is thus undoubtedly a political dimension to the novel, albeit one that is explored with even more subtlety than in the earlier post-war works.

In *How It Is*, the afterlife in the mud, characterized as it is by acts of torture, never suggests that human violence is a phenomenon that can be delimited, in the sense of it being consequent on a particular political context or a particular ideology. Rather, it is presented as characteristic of the human as such. At the same time, it can be read as a vision of everything that it is necessary for humanity to strive to move beyond, and, in that respect, it stands as a powerful critique of any relation of domination, not least those that are manifest at the political level in both nationalism and imperialism – those 'empires that are born and die', not least the British and the French empires.

The abstraction from a particular national-cultural context is taken even further in some of the shorter prose texts that Beckett wrote in the decades following the completion of *How It Is*. In those works, the setting cannot be located on any map, and it sits outside any particular history. The minimal action does not reflect any identifiable national culture, such affiliations and attachments being increasingly left behind. The comic attacks on cultural nationalism in the pre-war works, as well as the national-cultural disorientations of the prose and drama written in the immediate post-war years, give way in the later prose fiction to an exploration of the human beyond any kind of national or cosmopolitan context.

That rethinking, already evident in *How It Is*, continues in a project that Beckett commenced in English in August 1964 under the working title 'Fancy Dying'. Although he would abandon this project as a longer work of prose fiction, it did result in a number of shorter texts, including the English *All Strange Away* (which he also abandoned, in early 1965) and the French version of *Imagination Dead Imagine* (completed in March 1965). In those two works the setting cannot be located geographically, the figures described are shorn of national-cultural markers, and the action is so minimal as to be scarcely perceptible. The two texts describe figures in almost featureless closed spaces. They are re-imaginings of human life with all national-cultural attachments removed; in other words, a new vision of the human where the geometrical replaces the cultural.

In the final part of *All Strange Away*, entitled 'Diagram', a minimal 'womanly' figure is described within a small rotunda. The body of this figure is stripped of almost all features: 'Long black hair and lashes gone and puckered breast no details to add to these for the moment save normal neck with hint of cords and jugular and black bottomless eye' (Beckett, 2010e, 84). As for the mind, with the 'fancy dead', its only content is a single memory of 'felicity' – an abstract 'lying side by side' – and dreams of 'demons not yet imagined' (84). There are, however, still some proper names in *All Strange Away*: Jolly and Draeger (or Praeger), Emmo and Emma. There is also one reference to a recognizable place: the Pantheon in Rome. The minimal utterances that are imagined evoke a Christian cultural context: 'Mother mother, Mother in heaven, Mother of God, God in heaven, combinations with Christ and Jesus' (78). The 'ancient Greek philosophers' are also mentioned, with Diogenes the Cynic being singled out (78–9). This residual culture is that of the West, not that of a particular nation-state.

Even those residual cultural references are absent in *Imagination Dead Imagine*, which opens with the negation of any natural landscape, let alone any national-cultural realm: 'Islands, waters, azure, verdure, one glimpse and vanished, endlessly, omit' (Beckett, 2010e, 87). That natural setting is replaced by 'a plain rotunda, all white in the whiteness' (87). Within this placeless place, there are two white bodies, stripped not only of all clothing but also of all national-cultural signifiers. They have no birthmarks of the kind borne by Murphy. All that can be said of them is that, for all their immobility, they are not asleep. They experience extreme heat and cold in the rotunda, they open their left eyes at 'incalculable intervals', they murmur, and they react with an 'infinitesimal shudder' to the 'eye of prey' that observes them (89). Both *All Strange Away* and *Imagination Dead Imagine* present the reader with naked figures located within a closed space. The spaces in which they find themselves are geometrically described and could never be seen as homes or homelands in any cultural sense. And yet, as Beckett would later make clear, those spaces are nonetheless refuges of a sort.

In the context of works such as *Imagination Dead Imagine* and his later prose fiction, *Assez* – the text that Beckett wrote in French between September and December 1965, and that was published in English translation under the title *Enough* – stands as something of an outlier. Rather than describing figures located within a closed space, it focuses on two journeying figures, is narrated by a female, and returns to a more familiar world, set as it is in a natural landscape. It helps to remind the reader that Beckett's trajectory was never a simple, mono-directional one. That said, *Enough* contains no proper nouns (aside from the astronomical), and there is nothing to help locate the narrative within a particular national-cultural context. With *The Lost Ones*, also begun in late 1965, Beckett returned to the description of figures in a closed space, although on this occasion one that is far from peaceful. Written in French, only to be abandoned in May 1966, before a concluding paragraph was added in May 1970, *The Lost Ones* describes an 'abode' that is no genuine home to the 'lost bodies' that inhabit it. This abode that is anything but a place of security is a flattened cylinder with precisely stated dimensions: fifty metres round and sixteen metres high. It is an infernal realm in the sense that the lost ones who inhabit this cylinder are all in search of their particular lost other, but this search is a fruitless one, success being ruled out in principle from the outset. The cylinder is, we read: 'Vast enough for search to be in vain. Narrow enough for flight to be in vain' (Beckett, 2010e, 101). In other words, it is one more place of torture, like the mud of *How It Is*. It is also one more space without any national-cultural markers. The figures inhabiting it are truly citizens of nowhere, trapped in the cylinder but with no recollection of a home elsewhere. The absence of proper nouns achieves a level of abstraction that is fitting for this new vision of humanity, with the plurality of figures here reinforcing the sense of it being about humanity as a whole. Like the Nazi concentration camps, which were located outside any particular national culture while being the direct consequence of a rabid nationalist ideology, the abode of *The Lost Ones* is a place of suffering and of pointless exertion. Unlike those camps, however, the inhabitants of Beckett's abode have not been selected on account of any cultural or ethnic identity. They are an abstracted humanity, the dark side of the cosmopolitan universal.

In his next short prose text, *Ping*, originally written in French under the title *Bing*, and with a complex genetic history, Beckett continued his exploration of minimal figures in a realm stripped of national-cultural markers. Here the figure is a 'bare white body' located in a space of white walls and floor (Beckett, 2010e, 123). The only distinguishing marks are grey 'traces' or 'blurs', and a pair of light blue eyes that are 'almost white' (123). These barely perceptible 'signs' have, we are told, 'no meaning' (123). They are, moreover, residual, or, as Beckett puts it, 'unover', indicative of an irrecoverable and very different past. As for what happens to this barely perceptible figure in this white, featureless space, there are sounds ('murmurs') and there is movement, marked by a ping: 'Bare white body fixed ping fixed elsewhere' (123). Again, there are no proper nouns, nothing to locate the space on a map or to suggest any national-cultural affiliation for the figure. There are, however, signs of past violence: 'White scars invisible same white as flesh torn of old' (124). This suggests the idea of the space as a kind of refuge.

That the white space in *Ping* does indeed constitute a refuge of sorts, and that the figure inhabiting it is in fact a refugee, becomes clear in Beckett's next short prose work, *Lessness*, which was written in French (under the title *Sans*) and completed in August 1969. The working title for the English translation was 'Without', before being revised following a discussion between Beckett and his friend the Romanian-born philosopher E. M. Cioran, whose *The Trouble with Being Born* was published only a few years later (in 1973). In certain respects, *Lessness* is a culminating textual moment in Beckett's attempt to write such abstracted bodies in abstract spaces, stripped of all national-cultural signs. It is a particularly important work because it depicts the loss of any refuge, even those that seem more like prisons, such as the cylinder in *The Lost Ones*. In *Lessness*, there are none of the minimal references to be found in *How It Is* to Christian culture and to the 'humanities' that the narrator of that earlier work claims to have once possessed – his example being a knowledge of the French philosopher Nicolas Malebranche (1638–1715). The world of *Lessness* is featureless, history-less. It is again not a place that could be located on a political map of Europe, any more than could the realm of mud through which the narrator of *How It Is* crawls, the rotunda in *The Lost Ones*, or the white space in *Ping*.

Lessness thematizes the idea of the 'true refuge', the one that has been reached at 'long last' after 'so many false' (Beckett, 2010e, 129). That refuge is, however, no more than a ruin in the sand. It is not enclosed and does not protect the refugee. Beckett made this very clear in the blurb that, unusually, he agreed to write for the first UK edition of the text. There, he states that *Lessness* 'has to do with the collapse of some such refuge as that last attempted in *Ping* and with the ensuring situation of the refugee'. This brief statement casts considerable light not only on *Lessness* but on the earlier short prose works as well, revealing them to be attempts to explore experiences of refugees, who in those earlier texts have found forms of refuge. In *Lessness*, however – and this is why it is such an important text – Beckett turns to the experience of a life beyond the hope of any refuge. If the ruins are the only 'true refuge', they are also one that offers no protection and no way out: 'Scattered ruins ash grey all sides true refuge long last issueless' (130, 132). The irony here is that this so-called true refuge offers neither security nor freedom. The sense of entrapment in a state of exposure is also reinforced by the text's structure, since Beckett chose here for the first and only time to take a number of sentences (sixty in total) and to divide the text into two (unmarked) parts, with those sixty sentences being presented first in one 'disorder' and then in another. Those sentences are themselves the refuge as ruin that cannot be escaped, with the possibility being inscribed into the text of those sixty sentences being repeated in a varying order time and time again. Not one word in those sentences provides any sign of a national-cultural affiliation for the little body that is the only upright thing in this realm of grey ruins and grey sand.

Having pressed his exploration of the citizen of nowhere to such an extreme, it is perhaps unsurprising that Beckett should have taken a step back thereafter. Following the writing of a few other short prose texts that are also devoid of national-cultural markers, including 'For to End Yet Again' (written between November 1971 and summer 1972) and 'Still' (written between June and July 1972), Beckett completed *Company*, the first of three longer prose texts, in July 1979. While this work, written in English, again situates its figure in a space without any national-cultural markers – it is simply 'in the dark' – the voice that speaks of this figure's past life locates that past very clearly in Ireland. Unlike the majority of the prose texts from *How It Is* to 'Still', *Company* includes the recollection of a past that includes parents and concrete childhood experiences. One of these recollections is the following: 'A small boy you come out of Connolly's Stores holding your mother by the hand' (Beckett, 2009b, 5). Connolly's Stores was a shop located in Foxrock, the Dublin suburb where Beckett lived as a child, as is the Ballyogan Road, which is also mentioned in the text (14). Other proper names are also used. The midwife is identified as a Dr Hadden or Haddon (7). An acquaintance of his mother's is identified as a Mrs Coote (13). The make of the father's car is identified – a De Dion Bouton (8) – as is the magazine he likes to read: *Punch* (25). Dante returns, but as a named presence this time (40). Furthermore, Beckett resorts to a mocking of the Irish language that he had long since abandoned, writing of the figure on its back in the dark that it would understand nothing were it to be spoken to 'in Bantu or in Erse' (5). Significantly, Beckett retained all of these features in his French translation of *Company*, on no occasion seeking a French alternative (see Beckett, 1985). Why this reminder of Beckett's proud ignorance of the Irish language as a sign of his distance from Irish national culture? The answer arguably lies in his returning here to a world that he had left behind in his prose fiction of the 1960s and 1970s.

Company is, then, a bipolar work. On the one hand, it continues to explore the experience of those citizens of nowhere who populate many of the prose works from *How It Is* onwards. Here, that figure is on its back in the dark, hearing a voice speaking in the second person. On the other hand, there is the world of which that voice speaks, a world in which what purports to be the figure's past is recounted in fragmentary fashion. Unlike the present, that past can be situated very clearly on a political map, and includes the kinds of national-cultural markers to be found in Beckett's pre-war works. Significantly, however, *Company* ends by collapsing this bipolarity, reducing the entire idea of the voice recounting a concrete past to the status of a 'fable'. What remains following this act of linguistic negation is the figure 'alone' on its back in the dark – 'as you always were' (42). In other words, the text enacts the negation of all those signifiers of cultural-national attachment associated with its past, leaving nothing but one more minimal citizen of nowhere.

In *Ill Seen Ill Said*, the original French version of which he completed at the beginning of December 1981, after having worked on it for fifteen months, Beckett not only turned to the experience of a woman, as he had in *Enough*, but also avoided any of the national-cultural markers to be found in *Company*. That is not to say, however, that the text does not contain any political charge. Here the only proper names are those of Venus and Michelangelo. In the case of the latter, the reference in both the French and the English versions is to his 'regicide's bust' (Beckett, 1981, 55; 2009b, 68); that is, his marble bust of Brutus (1539–40), now in the Bargello museum in Florence. This passing reference clearly introduces a political dimension – the attempt to preserve a republic from autocratic rule through an act of violence. After all, Beckett could have chosen another work by Michelangelo. The potential relation between this and the woman's experience of being watched over by twelve sentinels is left for the reader to ponder.

In *Worstward Ho*, which he completed in March 1982, and which, after some preliminary efforts, he found it impossible to translate into French, Beckett avoided all proper names and all explicit national-cultural markers, even if the text's core idea is derived from Shakespeare's *King Lear*.[27] The power of negation here is such that all posited beings are immediately undone, or at least undone to the point where all that remains is the 'unlessable unworseable evermost almost void', so lacking in detail that it is barely utterable (Beckett, 2009b, 101). It takes the form of an old man and a child holding hands, and thus constituting a kind of community, and an old woman on her knees. These are truly citizens of nowhere, as is the mind in which these human figures appear. Ultimately, the three figures lose even their residual human form, becoming three pins, while the mind that perceives them is reduced to a pinhole, 'In dimmost dim. Vasts apart. At bounds of boundless void' (103). This is arguably Beckett's most extreme vision of his citizens of nowhere.

Turning to Beckett's later plays, one finds a similar trajectory towards an ever more extreme imagining of such unaffiliated figures. Following *Endgame*, the setting of Beckett's next major stage play, *Krapp's Last Tape* (written in English in early 1958), is another refuge – on this occasion, a 'den'. It is there that Krapp listens to tapes of his own past, before making one last recording. Like his namesake Victor Krap in *Eleutheria*, Krapp has sought to turn his back on humanity. In this, however, he has failed, as evidenced by the memories he

---

[27] As Dirk Van Hulle observes, Beckett noted down the following lines from *King Lear* in his 'Sottisier' notebook: 'The worst is not / So long as one can say, This is the worst' (Van Hulle in Beckett, 2009b, xiii).

stores on tape. These tapes, including the recording he makes during the play, not only demonstrate his failure to detach himself from his own past, but also show him to be inhabiting a world in which national-cultural affiliations remain in place. References to Connaught and to Croghan Hill in County Offaly make it clear that his life has been lived in Ireland, and while the location of his current refuge is not identified, there is no reason to doubt that it, too, is located there, given his recalling a recent visit to church for vespers. These identifiers are complicated, however, by Beckett's choice of proper names that speak to the play's thematizing of the opposition between light and dark.[28] Krapp recalls, for instance, a Bianca who lived on Kedar Street (this street name being an anagram of 'darke'), as well as a Miss McGlome, whose name suggests gloaming, or dusk (Beckett, 2009f, 6). In the French translation, these proper names are preserved, with no attempt being made to relocate the action to France. The plays on Kedar/darke and Glome/gloaming thus remain linguistic aliens in the French version. The key point here is that, just as Krapp remains, for all his cynicism, tied to his past, and in particular to the memory of a lover, so he is a figure whose detachment from any national-cultural context is far from complete. Indeed, it is less complete than that of the characters in *Endgame*.

This non-detachment is even more obviously the case in Beckett's first radio play, *All That Fall*, which he wrote in August and September 1956, while completing *Endgame*, and before the writing of *Krapp's Last Tape*. A connection between *All That Fall* and *Krapp's Last Tape* is established through their both including a reference to the novel *Effie Briest* (1895) by the German writer Theodor Fontane (Beckett, 2009a, 21; 2009f, 11). Tellingly, in *All That Fall* Beckett cannot resist returning to his longstanding bugbear, the Irish language. In the play, Mr Rooney recalls being led 'to the men's, or Fir as they call it now, from Vir Viris I suppose, the V becoming F, in accordance with Grimm's Law' (Beckett, 2009a, 27). What is striking here, however, is less the noting of the nationalist change of language (from English to Irish) following Irish independence, than Beckett's insisting on the connection between Irish and Latin in the case of the word for man: the Latin word *vir* meaning 'man' or 'hero', and being at the root of the English word 'virile'. The linguistic point being made here is that the Irish language is not pure; it is, like any language, a heterogeneous thing, to cite Defoe on the 'true-born Englishman'. National-cultural purity is, like linguistic purity, a myth, and a particularly dangerous one.

Beckett's next major play, *Happy Days*, written in English between October 1960 and May 1961, marks a significant step in Beckett's engagement with questions of national-cultural affiliation through its non-realist stage

---

[28] On this theme, see Knowlson (1972, passim; 1992, xxi–xxv).

image: a woman (Winnie) embedded in a low mound. This was Beckett's first attempt in the theatre to have a setting akin to those in his fiction from *How It Is* onwards, one that evokes the infernal or purgatorial settings in Dante's *Divine Comedy*. That said, national-cultural markers are not reduced to degree zero, for there are references to Christian culture in the play, and, more subtly, to European literary, philosophical, and musical culture, including Aristotle, William Shakespeare (*Romeo and Juliet*), John Milton (*Paradise Lost*), and Franz Lehár's operetta *The Merry Widow* (1906). Winnie ends her prayer with the words 'For Jesus Christ sake Amen. [. . .] World without end Amen' (Beckett, 2010a, 5), and the play thematizes the 'heavenly' and the 'hellish' light, just as *Krapp's Last Tape* thematizes light and dark. *Happy Days* develops further the idea already present in *Krapp's Last Tape* of a present that is radically different from the past, one that is no longer locatable within any national-cultural context.

The past that is recalled in the English version of *Happy Days* includes people (Charlie Hunter, Mr Johnson or Johnston) and places (Borough Green, a small town in Kent, England) that belong to a world characterized by national-cultural affiliations. Here, the scene is English rather than Irish. This is reinforced not only through the allusions to the English literary canon (Shakespeare and Milton) and to a town in Kent, but also through Winnie's husband, Willie, sporting what is identified as a 'Battle of Britain' moustache (Beckett, 2010a, 36). This seemingly insignificant detail is one more of those subtle inscriptions of modern European history into Beckett's work, like the reference to Sedan in *Endgame*. It is all the more striking on account of the radical rupture between past and present worlds that is thematized in *Happy Days* through Winnie's repeated references to the 'old style'; that is, a reliance upon language and concepts that do not have any meaning in the present circumstances, concepts such as day and night, but also, one imagines, the Battle of Britain. Significantly, in the French translation, and unlike in *Krapp's Last Tape*, Beckett opted for French alternatives for the proper names – Charlie Hunter becoming Charlot Chassepot and Borough Green becoming Fougax-et-Barrineuf – while he simply dropped the 'Battle of Britain' reference in the description of Willie's moustache (Beckett, 1974, 21, 73).

The world inhabited by Winnie now is in no sense one that could be located on a political map or within the kind of national culture signified by Willie's moustache. The markers of national-cultural affiliation, and the history pertaining to them, are remnants of a world to which Winnie no longer belongs. To speak of them, it is necessary to rely upon the 'old style'. The language of a new style, appropriate to the realm in which Winnie now finds herself, is one that Beckett would seek to achieve in his dramatic works during the following decades. That new style would be one suited to the realm inhabited by his citizens of nowhere.

The rupture between a past characterized by national-cultural affiliations and a radically different present is at the heart of Beckett's next major play, *Play*, written in English in the summer of 1962. Here, his placing of the three characters in urns makes it clear that their present is an infernal afterlife, in which they are condemned endlessly to rehearse scenes from their past lives. The non-naturalness that in *Happy Days* is signalled by the bell that rings to initiate speech, is effected here through the light that shines on the three characters' faces, prompting speech. This is one more scene of torture, evocative of a prisoner's interrogation. The three characters no longer have names: they are simply First Woman, Second Woman, and Man. The past life to which they refer, however, includes references to the Riviera, Grand Canary, and Lipton's tea. It is another twentieth-century English world, one in which Willie's Battle of Britain moustache would fit right in. Beyond these markers of a national-cultural context now lost, there is in *Play* also an allusion to Beckett's own earlier work. The name of Second Woman's butler is Erskine, this being the name of one of the servants in Mr Knott's house in *Watt*. Beckett is signalling that his own earlier works, in which national-cultural affiliations were still present, are being increasingly left behind. As in *Happy Days*, so in *Play*, the world in which those national-cultural affiliations have any meaning belongs to the past. This point is made less clearly in the French translation, however, since Erskine becomes Frontin. In the short play *Come and Go*, written in English in early 1965, Beckett includes a reference to the characters' schooldays at Miss Wade's. But even this sole concrete reference disappears in the French translation, where it becomes 'chez les sœurs' (Beckett, 1972, 40). Translation itself often serves to continue the movement away from the national.

A decade later, in his next major stage play, *Not I* (written in English in March and April 1972), Beckett again relied upon an infernal or pseudo-purgatorial setting in which a figure is compelled to recount a past while also speaking of the strangeness of the present situation. Here, however, the more concrete signifiers of national-cultural affiliation are all but absent from the recounted past. Mouth's present is simply 'in the dark', featureless, the darkness being interrupted from time to time by a ray of light. As for the recollected past, her place of birth is identified as a 'godforsaken hole', but a proper name (the only one in the play) is also used: Croker's Acres, which Beckett identified as being adjacent to Leopardstown Racecourse, south of Dublin. The reference to a merciful God and the words 'God is love' also situate this past culturally. Again, Beckett creates two worlds: a past in which there are national-cultural signifiers (albeit very few), and a present from which they have been stripped away. The French translation again constitutes a movement away even from a nationally located past, Croker's Acres becoming 'la vaine patûre' (Beckett, 1974, 90).

Often seen as a companion piece to *Not I*, *That Time* (written in English between June 1974 and August 1975) is similarly divided between a past that can be located within a national-cultural context and a present from which all such context has been removed. Here, Listener is, like Mouth, in the dark, the three voices coming to him from two sides and above. Those voices speak of a world that is richer in national-cultural identifiers than is Mouth's. One of the voices refers to a portrait gallery, an architectural folly named Foley's Folly, and the Doric railway terminus of the Great Southern and Eastern.[29] As for cultural references, another voice refers to 'that old Chinaman long before Christ born with long white hair' (Beckett, 2009f, 101). Commentators have suggested that the portrait gallery may be London's National Portrait Gallery, and that the railway terminus is Harcourt Street Station in Dublin, which opened in 1859 as the terminus for the Dublin–Bray (County Wicklow) line, and was closed down in 1958. As for the white-bearded Chinaman, he has been identified as the ancient Chinese philosopher Lao Tzu (604–531 BCE). Importantly, however, these national-cultural identifications, while possible, are less concrete than those in, for instance, *Happy Days*. The trajectory is thus clear. While Beckett continues here to contrast a culturally locatable past with an unlocatable present, the specificity of the former has been weakened and requires a greater level of decoding. One needs a knowledge of Beckett's own biography in order to be able to place that past in Dublin and London.

In the stage plays that he wrote after *That Time*, in which he continued to explore experiences of a recollected life, the national-cultural markers are not only absent from the present but also increasingly absent from the recollected past. In other words, these late citizens of nowhere were always already such. In *Footfalls* (written in English between March and December 1975), the only proper names are those of May and Amy (these being anagrams of each other) and Mrs Winter, whose name (like that of Miss McGlome in *Krapp's Last Tape*) has obvious thematic implications. As for May's past, as recounted by the voice of her mother, its culture is clearly Christian. It includes a scene in a church, 'His poor arm' being the arm of Christ on the Cross, symbolized in the church's architecture. Moreover, Beckett explained that he had chosen lacrosse as the sport once played by May on account of its verbal association with the Cross on which Christ died. In the French translation, this allusion is partially retained

---

[29] Foley becomes Fourier in the French version of *That Time* (see Beckett, 1986, 12). For a French reader, the name is most likely to evoke the figure of François Marie Charles Fourier (1772–1837), one of the founders of utopian socialism and a confirmed internationalist. Less well known is the French mathematician and theorist Jean-Baptiste Joseph Fourier (1768–1830).

through lacrosse becoming 'ce jeu du ciel and de l'enfer' (that game of heaven and hell) (Beckett, 1978, 11). When asked about his reliance upon Christian images in many of his works, Beckett explained that Christianity was a 'mythology' with which he was familiar, and that it would be quite wrong to see him as in any sense a Christian writer. While constituting a cultural limitation, his use of Christian imagery does not locate the settings within a particular national culture.

As we have seen, in *Happy Days*, *Play*, *Not I*, and *That Time*, the recollected past does bear national-cultural markers, suggesting a degree of national-cultural belonging. In contrast, in each of those plays the present is stripped of such markers, and is the dark space inhabited by Beckett's citizens of nowhere. In the short stage plays that he wrote thereafter, from *A Piece of Monologue* (written in English in autumn 1977, with the working title 'Gone') to *What Where* (written in French in early 1983), even the recollected past is stripped of such national-cultural affiliations. The past evoked in *A Piece of Monologue* is as lacking in such affiliations as are the photographs of Speaker's parents: 'There was father. That grey void. There mother. That other' (Beckett, 2009f, 118). In *Rockaby* (written in English in spring/summer 1980), the present is reduced to a figure in a rocking chair in the dark, while the life recollected by Voice is lacking in any details that could place it within a national culture. There is only a window, a window blind, a rocking chair, and a stair. All here is nondescript, with even the modifiers being in short supply. The stair is 'steep', the eyes are 'famished', the days are 'long'.

Ohio Impromptu (which he wrote in English in only a few days at the end of November 1981) is an outlier among these late plays in its including references to a very specific location. The recollected world is Parisian, as evidenced by the reference to the unnamed figure wearing a Latin Quarter hat and his moving to a single room from which he had a view of the Isle of Swans – that is, the Île aux Cygnes, a small, uninhabited, artificial island on the Seine in Paris's fifteenth arrondissement.[30] This reference is notable not least because in 1889 a quarter-scale replica of the statue *Liberty Enlightening the World* (better known as the Statue of Liberty) was erected on the Isle of Swans. Buried here is an allusion to one of Beckett's abiding themes: freedom, with a distinctly political dimension to it on this occasion.

That political dimension is much more clearly in evidence in Beckett's final two stage plays, *Catastrophe* and *What Where*. The political in *Catastrophe* is in no small part contextual. The play was written in French in early 1982, and

---

[30] In the French version, this hat becomes 'un grand chapeau de rapin' (Beckett, 1986, 61), a *rapin* being a bohemian artist.

dedicated to the Czech writer Václav Havel, who at the time was in prison on account of his political activities in what was then Communist Czechoslovakia. The action within the play – a rehearsal for a dramatic performance – thematizes oppression and forms of resistance to it, and includes one explicitly political reference: the Director tells his female Assistant to hurry up because he has a 'caucus' to attend (Beckett, 2009f, 144), this being a term (originating in the United States) for a political meeting. While this reference points away from Europe to the New World, that is not the case in the original French, 'caucus' translating 'comité' (Beckett, 1986, 75). Among the most well-known political *comités* (committees) in French history are the Committee of General Security (*Comité de sûreté générale*) and the Committee of Public Safety (*Comité de salut public*), which together oversaw the Reign of Terror following the French Revolution of 1789. The historical overtones here are thus considerably more disturbing in the original French version of the play.

The level of abstraction is even greater in *What Where* (written in French and completed in spring 1983). Here, Beckett continues to explore the theme of oppression and resistance that was addressed in *Catastrophe*. In *What Where*, this takes the form of a sequence of off-stage acts of torture, when each of the figures is in turn given 'the works', to try to make them confess some undisclosed information. There is nothing in *What Where*, however, to make this explicitly political, and the names of the four dramatis personae (Bam, Bem, Bim, Bom) recall those of earlier works, including *How It Is*, in which the figure of Pim is tortured. These figures are thus citizens of nowhere who continue to suffer outside any political context. Their not belonging to any identifiable national culture proves to be no liberation. Genuine freedom – arguably Beckett's most abiding theme – remains unachieved. While the figures in his late plays may belong nowhere, and may thus have escaped the confines of any national culture, they do not find themselves in a place where they can finally enjoy a freedom of either mind or body.

A trajectory very similar to that in Beckett's later stage plays is also observable in his plays for radio and television. As we have seen, in his first radio play, *All That Fall*, Beckett not only opts for an Irish setting, but also includes a comment on the Irish language that challenges the idea that it is free from Latin influence in the way that Fichte believed that the German language was untainted by the neo-Latin languages (above all, French). By the time of *Cascando* (written in French between December 1961 and January 1962), however, all such antagonistic engagements with national-cultural specificities have disappeared. The only proper name in *Cascando* is that of Woburn, whose movements (recounted by Voice) are those of a refugee. He goes down to a shore, climbs into a boat, and sets out to sea: 'heading nowhere ... for the island ... then no more ... elsewhere ... anywhere ... heading anywhere' (Beckett, 2009a, 90). Stateless, homeless, fleeing (not least from the voice that is seeking to capture him), Woburn is a minimalist, decontextualized embodiment of the Beckettian refugee.

In the late plays for television, it is not the refugee but rather figures in enclosed spaces stripped of all national-cultural specificities that become the focus, mirroring Beckett's treatment of such spaces in his prose works of the period. There is, for instance, the unnamed figure in a room in *Ghost Trio* (written from 1975 to 1976), awaiting a female figure who never arrives, in a radically minimalist reworking of *Godot*. Here, all is 'Shades of grey' (Beckett, 2009a, 125). While the title and the last lines of '... *but the clouds* ...' (written in October and November 1976) are taken from W. B. Yeats's poem 'The Tower', the setting is as abstracted as that in *Ghost Trio*. The 'little sanctum' into which the male figure withdraws could be anywhere and nowhere. He is, like the male figure of *Ghost Trio*, isolated and alone, one more delocalized citizen of nowhere.

5 Conclusion

Arguably the greatest political lesson of the century in which Beckett lived and wrote was that nationalism, the privileging of one nation's interests and culture over those of others, and the shaping of a particular national culture in antagonistic relation to other national cultures, will almost inevitably result in violence. Given his sustained resistance to – and, in his post-war works, his undoing of – cultural-national affiliations, as well as his commitment to producing a bilingual oeuvre, it might seem justifiable to see Beckett as the perfect example of what, in *Beyond Good and Evil* (1886), Friedrich Nietzsche describes as the 'good European'. According to Nietzsche, the good European is 'an essentially supra-national and nomadic type of person' who is acutely aware of 'the pathological manner in which nationalist nonsense has alienated and continues to alienate the peoples of Europe from each other' (Nietzsche, 2002, 133, 148). Unlike the oeuvre of a writer such as Stefan Zweig, however, Beckett's post-war works are not ultimately the expression of a good Europeanism in Nietzsche's sense. His prose fiction and plays neither represent nor champion internationalism and the idea of a shared European home. And neither did Beckett seek to become a member of Voltaire's 'great republic of cultivated minds'. Rather, his post-war works cast a critical light upon all political identifications, not only national affiliations but also international, cosmopolitan ones. Indeed, they insist upon a difference between the supra-national and the nomadic that is not present in Nietzsche, for the nomad is to be distinguished from the cosmopolitan in that the former has no home, no imagined community, whereas the latter claims to be at home everywhere.

In his post-war works, when he was writing in both French and English, this nomadic quality manifested itself not least in Beckett's movement between languages. As various studies of Beckett's bilingual oeuvre have demonstrated, the relation between first and second language, and between original and translation, is not sustainable in Beckett's case. The relation between versions is more complex, and less unidirectional, than that.[31] Furthermore, his concerted engagement with the German translations of his works, as well as his directing of his plays in German at the Schillertheater, Berlin, in the 1960s and 1970s, weakens any sense of a binary structure of Ireland/France and English/French. Ultimately, Beckett is no more an Irish writer than he is a French writer, for such national ascriptions are increasingly subject to the pressure of a perpetual migrancy in his work, captured most effectively, perhaps, in that single, recurrent syllable 'on', from its appearance at the end of *The Unnamable* to its central role in one of his last works, *Worstward Ho*. And neither is he a European nor indeed a cosmopolitan writer, in the sense of his work affirming either Europe or the world as a homeland.

Beckett's commitment to multilingualism is in part a mode of resistance to cultural nationalism. He challenges the privileging of any national language, and indeed the very idea of a national language. He shows how languages are never pure, any more than are nations. In this, his approach differs markedly from those taken by two of the writers who meant most to him: Dante and Joyce. Dante turned away from Latin (as the language of the cosmopolitan elite) and sought a new literary language in the Tuscan dialect, this marking a significant early step towards the idea of national languages and literatures. As for Joyce, he sought in *Finnegans Wake* to create a new form of English that, while it embraced multilingualism, was nonetheless his alone. Beckett's poor imitations of Joyce in parts of *Dream of Fair to Middling Women* make this clear. As Beckett himself acknowledged to his publisher, his first literary efforts stank of Joyce (see Beckett, 2009g, 81). Beckett's linguistic migration from English to French shortly after the Second World War was not a shifting of national-linguistic allegiances. Rather, it opened up a new space between languages in which the writer remains, as it were, a word migrant, his language an impure, heterogeneous thing. This experience of linguistic migrancy is enacted in Beckett's own self-translations, and is particularly striking in the genetic history of those acts of self-translation, as evidenced by the Beckett Digital Manuscript Project.

---

[31] Following Fitch's landmark work (1988), there have been numerous other fine studies of Beckett's practice as a self-translator, and of the (often complex) relationship between versions in different languages. These studies (including the volumes in the Beckett Digital Manuscript Project) have only deepened the sense that the original/translation model is inadequate as an approach to Beckett's oeuvre.

For all its apparent darkness, for all its unremitting focus on suffering, weakness, and loss, Beckett's oeuvre stands as one of the great literary testaments to the importance of our thinking first and foremost not about what it means to have been born in one place rather than another, or to speak one language rather than another, or to inhabit one culture rather than another, but what it means to be a human being in the most basic, impoverished sense, stripped of all national-cultural attachments. What remains is a figure of the human as one finds it in *Lessness*: a little body in a landscape where ruins are the sole refuge. That is Beckett's version of what Giorgio Agamben (1998) terms *homo sacer* – the human as 'bare life'. As Agamben makes clear, this bare life is a biopolitical category. One might thus go so far as to say that, if there any are messages in Beckett's work (something that he would certainly have denied), then one of them is that all national-cultural identifications are disastrously mythic in nature, but that the alternative to these identifications is not a cosmopolitan conception of humanity stemming from the Enlightenment. In his reflections on Europe, Jacques Derrida argues that, paradoxical as it might seem, 'Nationalism and cosmopolitanism have always gotten along well together' (Derrida, 1992, 48). Beckett appears to have shared this scepticism towards the idea of cosmopolitanism as a genuine alternative to nationalism. As we have seen, the protagonist in *Eleutheria* turns his emaciated back on humanity. The Beckettian refugee is at some level also fleeing the human and all imagined human communities.

If Beckett does appeal to an idea of humanity, then it is neither national nor cosmopolitan, but rather what, in the radio script 'The Capital of the Ruins' (1946), he terms a 'humanity in ruins'. In that text, Beckett reflected on the significance of what had happened at the Irish Red Cross Hospital established at the end of the Second World War at Saint-Lô, a town in Normandy that had been almost completely destroyed by Allied bombing in June 1944. Beckett acknowledged that the national identification of the hospital was likely to be an enduring one. 'I think', he wrote, 'that to the end of its hospital days it will be called the Irish Hospital, and after that the huts, when they have been turned into dwellings, the Irish huts. I mention this possibility, in the hope that it will give general satisfaction' (Beckett, 1995, 278). One can assume that by this he meant general satisfaction to the Irish. But he did not stop there, for he then took a decisive step beyond such national affiliations. Having acknowledged the possibility that the hospital and the huts would in all likelihood remain Irish, he added another possibility:

> I may perhaps venture to mention another, more remote but perhaps of greater import in certain quarters, I mean the possibility that some of those who were

in Saint-Lô will come home [to Ireland] realising that they got at least as good
as they gave, that they got indeed what they could hardly give, a vision and
a sense of a time-honoured conception of humanity in ruins, and perhaps even
an inkling of the terms in which our condition is to be thought again. These
will have been in France. (278)

In other words, however proud Ireland might be of what it had offered to
assist the French, it received as much as it gave, and what it received was
nothing less than a nominalist conception of the human, in the sense that it is
homeless.

Beckett's rejection both of national-cultural and cosmopolitan affiliations and
homelands is rooted in his profoundly nominalist outlook. In the 1930s, as part
of his philosophical self-education, he acquainted himself with the tradition of
philosophical nominalism. His appreciation of nominalism is reflected in his
well-known letter in July 1937 to Axel Kaun, shortly after his return from Nazi
Germany. In that letter, Beckett imagined the possibility of a 'literature of the
non-word' as the alternative to what he saw as Joyce's 'apotheosis of the word'
(Beckett, 2009g, 519–20). In so doing, he referred to the need for 'some form of
nominalistic irony', which would undo the generalizations upon which identifi-
catory and conceptual thinking depend, and thus also undo the meanings
generated by that kind of thinking (520). Among the many examples of
Beckett's nominalism, one of the most often cited is the passage concerning
the pot in *Watt*. Although that pot is 'almost a pot', the perceived object never
quite accords with the concept of a pot, and this troubles Watt deeply, since he is
anything but a nominalist (Beckett, 2009j, 67). This well-known example is
significant not least because it is not simply an instance of philosophical
nominalism, for there is a political dimension to the passage, too. While in
Nazi Germany, Beckett had learned of the Nazis' '*Eintopf* Sundays' initiative,
when Germans were supposed to eat a cheap stew of meat, potatoes, and other
vegetables to support the idea of the unity of the German nation (see Van Hulle
and Verhulst, 2020, 39). This idea of the *Eintopf* (literally, 'one pot') was
introduced by Beckett into the manuscript of *Watt*, only later to be removed.
Similarly, when translating the phrase 'plat unique' in *Molloy* (Beckett, 1971,
87), he again opted initially for 'Eintopf', before revising this to 'mess'
(BDMP4, ET2, 63r; Beckett, 2009h, 53).[32] Furthermore, as Emilie Morin has
observed, by associating the Nazi *Eintopf* with Irish stew, Beckett controver-
sially established a connection between Irish and German nationalism.[33] The

[32] See O'Reilly, Van Hulle, and Verhulst (2017, 349–50).
[33] On Beckett's engagement with the idea of the *Eintopf*, see Van Hulle and Verhulst (2020, 39–40)
and Morin (2009, 229).

kind of philosophical nominalism to be found in *Watt*, and indeed throughout Beckett's later work, is thus also a form of political nominalism.

Seen more broadly, Beckett's political nominalism militates not only against all national-cultural affiliations, but also against both cosmopolitanism and humanism. It is for this reason that he insists on the idea of humanity in ruins. If there is a cosmopolitanism in his work, then it, too, is a cosmopolitanism in ruins. By that is to be understood a shared homelessness, everywhere. The negative charge here is crucial. For while Beckett's rejection of all forms of nationalism is clear, it is far from evident that his idea of humanity in ruins, or a homeless humanity, is anything to be celebrated as a positive value. Values in Beckett's work – including that of humanity in ruins – would seem only ever to be negative. As soon as they become positive, they become mythic. With regard to nationalism, this means that while his work stands as one of the most telling rejections of the nationalist myth in the twentieth century, it never becomes the affirmation of the cosmopolitan. To take up a figure from Beckett's first book publication (his short monograph on Proust), his work carries us into the 'core of the eddy' (Beckett, 1965, 65–6), where concepts such as nationalism, cosmopolitanism, and humanism are subjected to the corrosive power of the negative.

The negative charge that we have seen associated with the inscriptions of Irish culture and history in his pre-war works, and then also of French culture and history in his post-war works, signals Beckett's critical distance from both of those cultures when conceived in terms of cultural nationalism. Rather than seeking to identify with some form of French culture, in place of an unpalatable Irish cultural nationalism, Beckett sought to locate his figures and his work in a zone of displacement or unbelonging between cultures. His oeuvre is thus not *both* Irish *and* French, but *neither* Irish *nor* French. This neither/nor logic – which includes his attitude to national cultures – is articulated with particular clarity in the short prose text 'neither' (1976): 'as between two refuges whose doors once neared gently close, once turned away from gently part again' (Beckett, 2010e, 167). When those refuges are national cultures, they are traps. Beckett's work subtly reminds us that these traps are responsible for many of the horrors of modern European history, from Napoleon to Hitler, for, as we have seen, while Beckett's focus is often on the Irish scene, his works contain subtle references to Napoleon's disastrous invasion of Russia in 1812, the Franco-Prussian War of 1870–1, and the Nazi conquest of much of Continental Europe. Each of those moments in modern European history was owing to an unbridled nationalism. Beckett's objection to cultural nationalism in Ireland needs to be seen within his awareness of that broader context. It is striking, for instance, that the murderous Lemuel in *Malone Dies*, who in the

French manuscript was originally called Samuel, claims that his parents were 'probably Aryan' (Beckett, 2010b, 95–6).[34]

While Beckett's work is undoubtedly unique, the experience of unbelonging that it explores does have parallels in twentieth-century European literature. Some of the other major writers of the period also responded to the horrors of modern history in a manner that, while recognizing the role of nationalism therein, did not endorse cosmopolitanism. Both Paul Celan and W. G. Sebald, in their very different ways, sought to capture an experience of unbelonging that bears comparison with that in Beckett's post-war fiction and drama. And it is no coincidence that both Celan and Sebald thought highly of Beckett's work. Like Beckett, they not only captured the traumatic nature of modern history but also resisted both national and cosmopolitan affiliations, preferring to remain, as it were, out in the cold. Difficult as it was, they, like Beckett, seem to have believed that in order to be true to their art, it was necessary to resist such lures. In Celan's case, Nazism was responsible for the death of his parents. In Beckett's, it was responsible for the death of close friends, including Alfred Péron, to whom he dedicated the French translation of *Murphy*.

Ultimately, Beckett's attitude to cultural nationalism is not that hard to understand. More challenging is his resistance to cosmopolitanism, and his preference for an idea of humanity in ruins. And more challenging still is his insistence that it is through a reflection upon the idea of humanity in ruins that, as he puts it, our condition may be thought again. It is just such a reimaging of our human condition, beyond both nationalism and cosmopolitanism, that Beckett undertakes in his post-war work, and it is not least for that reason that his work remains such a vital, and such a disturbing, presence for us today.

---

[34] On Beckett's play on Éireann/Aryan, see Mooney (2011, 153). On the revision of Samuel to Lemuel in the French manuscript, see Van Hulle and Verhulst (2017b, 237).

Bibliography

Ackerley, C. J. (2005), *Obscure Locks, Simple Keys: The Annotated 'Watt'*, Tallahassee, FL: Journal of Beckett Studies Books.

Agamben, Giorgio (1998), *Homo Sacer: Sovereign Power and Bare Life*, trans. Daniel Heller-Roazen, Stanford: Stanford University Press.

Anderson, Benedict (2016), *Imagined Communities: Reflections on the Origin and Spread of Nationalism*, revised edition, London and New York: Verso.

Beckett, Samuel (1965), *Proust and Three Dialogues*, London: Calder & Boyars.

Beckett, Samuel (1971), *Molloy*, Paris: Les Éditions de Minuit.

Beckett, Samuel (1972), *Comédie et actes divers*, Paris: Les Éditions de Minuit.

Beckett, Samuel (1974), *Oh les beaux jours, suivi de Pas moi*, Paris: Les Éditions de Minuit.

Beckett, Samuel (1978), *Pas, suivi de quatre esquisses*, Paris: Les Éditions de Minuit.

Beckett, Samuel (1981), *Mal vu mal dit*, Paris: Les Éditions de Minuit.

Beckett, Samuel (1983), *Disjecta: Miscellaneous Writings and a Dramatic Fragment*, ed. Ruby Cohn, London: John Calder.

Beckett, Samuel (1985), *Compagnie*, Paris: Les Éditions de Minuit.

Beckett, Samuel (1986), *Catastrophe et autres dramaticules*, Paris: Les Éditions de Minuit.

Beckett, Samuel (1987), *Nouvelles et Textes pour rien*, Paris: Les Éditions de Minuit.

Beckett, Samuel (1992), *Dream of Fair to Middling Women*, ed. Eoin O'Brien and Edith Fournier, Dublin: The Black Cat Press.

Beckett, Samuel (1995), *The Complete Short Prose, 1929–1989*, ed. S. E. Gontarski, New York: Grove Press.

Beckett, Samuel (1996), *Eleutheria*, trans. Barbara Wright, London: Faber and Faber.

Beckett, Samuel (2009a), *'All That Fall' and Other Plays for Radio and Screen*, with a Preface and Notes by Everett Frost, London: Faber and Faber.

Beckett, Samuel (2009b), *Company, Ill Seen Ill Said, Worstward Ho, Stirrings Still*, ed. Dirk Van Hulle, London: Faber and Faber.

Beckett, Samuel (2009c), *Endgame*, with a Preface by Rónán McDonald, London: Faber & Faber.

Beckett, Samuel (2009d), *'The Expelled', 'The Calmative', 'The End', with 'First Love'*, ed. Christopher Ricks, London: Faber and Faber.

Beckett, Samuel (2009e), *How It Is*, ed. Édouard Magessa O'Reilly, London: Faber and Faber.

Beckett, Samuel (2009f), *'Krapp's Last Tape' and Other Shorter Plays*, with a Preface by S. E. Gontarski, London: Faber and Faber.

Beckett, Samuel (2009g), *The Letters of Samuel Beckett, Vol. I: 1929–1940*, ed. Martha Dow Fehsenfeld and Lois More Overbeck, Cambridge: Cambridge University Press.

Beckett, Samuel (2009h), *Molloy*, ed. Shane Weller, London: Faber and Faber.

Beckett, Samuel (2009i), *Murphy*, ed. J. C. C. Mays, London: Faber and Faber.

Beckett, Samuel (2009j), *Watt*, ed. C. J. Ackerley, London: Faber and Faber.

Beckett, Samuel (2010a), *Happy Days: A Play in Two Acts*, with a Preface by James Knowlson, London: Faber and Faber.

Beckett, Samuel (2010b), *Malone Dies*, ed. Peter Boxall, London: Faber and Faber.

Beckett, Samuel (2010c), *Mercier and Camier*, ed. Seán Kennedy, London: Faber and Faber.

Beckett, Samuel (2010d), *More Pricks Than Kicks*, ed. Cassandra Nelson, London: Faber and Faber.

Beckett, Samuel (2010e), *'Texts for Nothing' and Other Shorter Prose, 1950–1976*, ed. Mark Nixon, London: Faber and Faber.

Beckett, Samuel (2010f), *The Unnamable*, ed. Steven Connor, London: Faber & Faber.

Beckett, Samuel (2010g), *Waiting for Godot*, with a Preface by Mary Bryden, London: Faber & Faber.

Beckett, Samuel (2011), *The Letters of Samuel Beckett, Vol. II: 1941–1956*, ed. George Craig, Martha Dow Fehsenfeld, Dan Gunn, and Lois More Overbeck, Cambridge: Cambridge University Press.

Beckett, Samuel (2014), *The Letters of Samuel Beckett, Vol. III: 1957–1965*, ed. George Craig, Martha Dow Fehsenfeld, Dan Gunn, and Lois More Overbeck, Cambridge: Cambridge University Press.

Beckett, Samuel (2016), *The Letters of Samuel Beckett, Vol. IV: 1966–1989*, ed. George Craig, Martha Dow Fehsenfeld, Dan Gunn, and Lois More Overbeck, Cambridge: Cambridge University Press.

Boswell, James (1958), *The Journal of a Tour to the Hebrides with Samuel Johnson*, London: Dent.

Boswell, James (1980), *Life of Johnson*, ed. R. W. Chapman, The World's Classics, Oxford: Oxford University Press.

Cicero, Marcus Tullius (1945), *Tusculan Disputations*, trans. J. E. King, revised edition, Loeb Classical Library, Volume 18, Cambridge, MA: Harvard University Press.

Clare, David (2018), 'Anglo-Irish "Distortion": Double Exposure in Francis Bacon's Portraits and Samuel Beckett's *The Old Tune*', *New Hibernian Review*, 22:1, pp. 102–19.

Defoe, Daniel (1997), *'The True-Born Englishman' and Other Writings*, ed. P. N. Furbank and W. R. Owens, Penguin Classics, Harmondsworth: Penguin.

Derrida, Jacques (1992), *The Other Heading: Reflections on Today's Europe*, trans. Pascale-Anne Brault and Michael B. Nass, Bloomington: Indiana University Press.

Ellmann, Richard (1987), *Four Dubliners: Wilde, Yeats, Joyce, and Beckett*, London: Hamish Hamilton.

Fichte, Johann Gottlieb (2008), *Addresses to the German Nation*, ed. and trans. Gregory Moore, Cambridge: Cambridge University Press.

Fichte, Johann Gottlieb (2012), *The Closed Commercial State*, trans. Anthony Curtis Adler, Albany: State University of New York Press.

Fitch, Brian T. (1988), *Beckett and Babel: An Investigation into the Status of the Bilingual Work*, Toronto: University of Toronto Press.

Gibson, Andrew (2010), *Samuel Beckett, Critical Lives*, London: Reaktion Books.

Graham, Alan (2015), '"So much Gaelic to me": Beckett and the Irish Language', *Journal of Beckett Studies*, 24:2, pp. 163–79.

Herder, Johann Gottfried von (1800), *Outlines of a Philosophy of the History of Man [Ideen zur Philosophie der Geschichte der Menschheit]*, trans. T. Churchill, London: J. Johnson.

Hill, Leslie (1990), *Samuel Beckett's Fiction: In Different Words*, Cambridge: Cambridge University Press.

Houston, Lloyd Meadhbh (2018), '"Sterilization of the Mind and Apotheosis of the Litter": Beckett, Censorship, and Fertility', *Review of English Studies*, 62:290, pp. 546–64.

Joyce, James (1991), *A Portrait of the Artist as a Young Man*, New York: Alfred A. Knopf.

Joyce, James (2000a), *Dubliners*, with an Introduction and Notes by Terence Brown, London: Penguin.

Joyce, James (2000b), *Finnegans Wake*, with an Introduction by Seamus Deane, London: Penguin.

Kafka, Franz (1995), *Stories 1904–1924*, trans. J. A. Underwood, London: Abacus.

Kennedy, Seán (ed.) (2010), *Beckett and Ireland*, Cambridge: Cambridge University Press.

Kennedy, Seán (2019), 'Beckett, Censorship and the Problem of Parody', *Estudios Irlandeses*, 14:2, pp. 104–14.

Knowlson, James (1972), *Light and Dark in the Theatre of Samuel Beckett*, London: Turret Books.

Knowlson, James (ed.) (1992), *The Theatrical Notebooks of Samuel Beckett, Volume III: Krapp's Last Tape*, London: Faber and Faber.

Knowlson, James (1996), *Damned to Fame: The Life of Samuel Beckett*, London: Bloomsbury.

Knox, Robert (1850), *The Races of Men: A Fragment*, Philadelphia: Lea and Blanchard.

MacGreevy, Thomas (1945), *Jack B. Yeats: An Appreciation and an Interpretation*, Dublin: Victor Waddington Publications.

Monbron, Louis-Charles Fougeret de (2010), *Le Cosmopolite, ou le citoyen du monde*, ed. Édouard Langille, London: Modern Humanities Research Association.

Mooney, Sinéad (2011), *A Tongue Not Mine: Beckett and Translation*, Oxford: Oxford University Press.

Moorjani, Angela (2009), 'Whence Estragon?', *The Beckett Circle*, 32:2 (Fall), 7.

Morin, Emilie (2009), *Samuel Beckett and the Problem of Irishness*, Basingstoke: Palgrave Macmillan.

Morin, Emilie (2017), *Beckett's Political Imagination*, Cambridge: Cambridge University Press.

Nietzsche, Friedrich (2002), *Beyond Good and Evil: Prelude to a Philosophy of the Future*, ed. Rolf-Peter Horstmann and Judith Norman, trans. Judith Norman, Cambridge: Cambridge University Press.

Nixon, Mark (2011), *Samuel Beckett's German Diaries 1936–1937*, London and New York: Continuum.

O'Reilly, Édouard Magessa, Van Hulle, Dirk, and Verhulst, Pim (2017), *The Making of Samuel Beckett's 'Molloy'*, Brussels: University Press Antwerp; London: Bloomsbury Academic.

Pilling, John (2004), *A Companion to 'Dream of Fair to Middling Women'*, Tallahassee, FL: Florida State University Press; Journal of Beckett Studies Books.

Pinget, Robert (n.d.), 'Notre ami Samuel Beckett', typescript, Beckett International Foundation, University of Reading.

Rabaté, Jean-Michel (2020), *Beckett and Sade*, Cambridge: Cambridge University Press.

Rivarol, Antoine (2013), *Discours sur la universalité de la langue française, précédé de La Langue humaine par Gérard Dessons*, Paris: Éditions Manucius.

Robertson, Ritchie (2020), *The Enlightenment: The Pursuit of Happiness 1680–1790*, London: Allen Lane.

Rougemont, Denis de (1966), *The Idea of Europe*, trans. Norman Guterman, New York: The Macmillan Company; London: Collier-Macmillan Ltd.

Rousseau, Jean-Jacques (1997), *Considerations on the Government of Poland and on its Projected Reformation*; in *'The Social Contract' and Other Later Political Writings*, ed. and trans. Victor Gourevitch, Cambridge: Cambridge University Press, pp. 177–260.

Saint Victor, Hugh of (1991), *The Didascalicon of Hugh of Saint Victor: A Medieval Guide to the Arts*, New York: Columbia University Press.

Schopenhauer, Arthur (1974), *Parerga and Paralipomena: Short Philosophical Essays*, trans. E. F. J. Payne, 2 vols, Oxford: Clarendon Press.

Tonning, Erik (2014), *Modernism and Christianity*, Basingstoke: Palgrave Macmillan.

Van Hulle, Dirk, and Verhulst, Pim (2017a), *The Making of Samuel Beckett's 'En attendant Godot'/'Waiting for Godot'*, Brussels: University Press Antwerp; London: Bloomsbury Academic.

Van Hulle, Dirk, and Verhulst, Pim (2017b), *The Making of Samuel Beckett's 'Malone meurt'/'Malone Dies'*, Brussels: University Press Antwerp; London: Bloomsbury Academic.

Van Hulle, Dirk, and Verhulst, Pim (2020), 'Shifting Cultural Affinities in *Molloy*: A Genetic Bilingual Approach', in Thirthankar Chakraborty and Juan Luis Toribio Vazquez (eds.), *Samuel Beckett as World Literature*, New York: Bloomsbury Academic, pp. 29–43.

Van Hulle, Dirk, and Weller, Shane (2018), *The Making of Samuel Beckett's 'Fin de partie'/'Endgame'*, Brussels: University Press Antwerp; London: Bloomsbury Academic.

Voltaire (2005), *Candide, or Optimism*, trans. Theo Cuffe, London: Penguin.

Weller, Shane (2015), 'The Tone of Displacement: Samuel Beckett, Robert Pinget and the Art of Adaptation', in Mark Nixon and John Pilling (eds.), *On in Their Company: Essays on Beckett, with Tributes and Sketches*, Reading: Beckett International Foundation, pp. 25–44.

Weller, Shane (2018), 'For a Migrant Art: Samuel Beckett and Cultural Nationalism', *Journal of European Studies*, 2:48, pp. 168–82.

Weller, Shane (2020), 'Negative Anthropology: Beckett and Humanism', *Samuel Beckett Today/Aujourd'hui*, 32:2, pp. 161–75.

Weller, Shane (2021), *The Idea of Europe: A Critical History*, Cambridge: Cambridge University Press.

Winstanley, Adam (2014), '"Grâce aux excréments des citoyens": Beckett, Swift and the Coprophagic Economy of Ballyba', *Samuel Beckett Today/Aujourd'hui*, 26:1, pp. 91–105.

Yeats, W. B. (1989), *The Collected Works of W. B. Yeats, Volume I: The Poems*, ed. Richard Finneran, revised edition, New York: Macmillan Publishing Company.

Cambridge Elements ☰

Beckett Studies

Dirk Van Hulle
University of Oxford
Dirk Van Hulle is Professor of Bibliography and Modern Book History at the University of Oxford and director of the Centre for Manuscript Genetics at the University of Antwerp.

Mark Nixon
University of Reading
Mark Nixon is Associate Professor in Modern Literature at the University of Reading and the Co-Director of the Beckett International Foundation.

About the Series
This series presents cutting-edge research by distinguished and emerging scholars, providing space for the most relevant debates informing Beckett studies as well as neglected aspects of his work. In times of technological development, religious radicalism, unprecedented migration, gender fluidity, environmental and social crisis, Beckett's works find increased resonance. Cambridge Elements in Beckett Studies is a key resource for readers interested in the current state of the field.

Cambridge Elements ☰

Beckett Studies

Elements in the Series

Experimental Beckett: Contemporary Performance Practices
Nicholas E. Johnson and Jonathan Heron

Postcognitivist Beckett
Olga Beloborodova

Samuel Beckett's Geological Imagination
Mark Byron

Beckett and Sade
Jean-Michel Rabaté

*Beckett's Intermedial Ecosystems: Closed Space Environments across the Stage,
Prose and Media Works*
Anna McMullan

Samuel Beckett and Cultural Nationalism
Shane Weller

A full series listing is available at: www.cambridge.org/eibs

Printed in the United States
by Baker & Taylor Publisher Services